NEW Blueprint INTERMEDIATE

CW01583304

Elaine Walker & Steve Elsworth

Workbook

Longman

Contents

Unit 1

HOW GOOD IS YOUR ENGLISH?

Do the Blueprint check and find out.

TENSE CHECK: all tenses

1 Write the correct form of the verbs, choosing from all the tenses which you know.

Mark Pringle (be) .... two years older than his cousin Nick. After he left school, he (get) 1 .... a job with a music magazine. For the last two years he (work) 2 .... as a general reporter. 'I (like) 3 .... the work,' he says. 'Next year, I (probably go) 4 .... to New York to work as the American correspondent.'

Like Nick, Mark (go) 5 .... to a public school — Charterhouse — and he (not like) 6 .... it, either. 'I (be) 7 .... very pleased when I (leave) 8 .... two years ago. If I have any children, I (not send) 9 .... them to a public school, I (send) 10 .... them to a state school.'

Mark didn't go to University. 'I (not get) 11 .... very good grades in my 'A' Levels,' he says, 'but that's O.K., because I (not need) 12 .... good 'A' Level grades to do this job.'

At the moment, he (study) 13 .... Spanish and Portuguese. 'A lot of good music (come) 14 .... from South America, and after New York, I (want) 15 .... to go and live there for a few years.'

SENTENCE STRUCTURE: mixed structures

2 Choose the correct sentence endings.

I haven't ....

1 He's two years older ....
2 She's the same age ....
3 It was the most ....
4 She's been outside ....
5 He's been here since ....
6 I don't really like ....

A going to restaurants.
B been here before.
C as I am.
D than me.
E expensive suit in the shop.
F four o'clock.
G for two hours.

COMMUNICATION

3 Choose the correct response and write a) or b) in the box.

		Box	Responses
	I'm very thirsty.	b	a) So do I. b) So am I.
1	Would you like a sandwich?	a	a) I'd love one. b) I love one.
2	I don't like this very much.	a	a) So do I. b) Nor do I.
3	Do you agree?	a	a) No, I don't. b) No, I'm not.
4	Diana's got a new job.	b	a) Is she? b) Has she?
5	Have you got any money?	a	a) Only a few. b) Only a little.
6	Did she go early?	b	a) Yes, she went. b) Yes, she did.
7	Can Mike come too?	a	a) Yes, if he wants to. b) Yes, if he wanted to.
8	Will Mr Harrison be there?	b	a) No, he isn't. b) No, he won't.
9	Is the train in the station?	b	a) No, it went. b) No, it's gone.
10	Are you reading this book?	b	a) Yes, I am. b) Yes, I'm reading.

WORD FORMATION

4 Write the verbs connected with these nouns.

	annoyance	*annoy*
1	approval	
2	agreement	
3	education	
4	thought	
5	life	

WORD STRESS

5 Write these words with the stressed syllable in capital letters. Use a dictionary if you want to.

	student	*STUdent*			
1	university	UNIversity	6	magazine	MAGAzine
2	academic	ACAdemic	7	company	COMpany
3	opposite	OPPosite	8	computer	COMPuter
4	annoy	ANNOY	9	ridiculous	RIDIculous
5	musician	MUSIcian	10	education	EDUcation

Unit 2

GRAMMAR: present simple and present continuous

1 Write the correct form of the verbs, using the present simple or present continuous tenses.

She (have) ...has... a nice job in a bank.

1 They (study) ...are studing... hard for their exams at the moment.

2 He usually (play) ...plays... tennis on Wednesdays.

3 A lot of tourists (visit) ...visit... this place each year.

4 I'm afraid I (not understand) ...don't understand... .

5 (You / go out) ...Are you going out... tomorrow night?

6 Tom's not here, he (stay) ...'s staying... with Pat this week.

2 Mark Pringle is interviewing a singer about her work. Complete the interview with the correct form of the verbs, using the present simple or present continuous tenses.

(you / like) ...Do you like... the music business, Diana?

Oh yes, I (love) 1 ...love... it. I (like) 2 ...like... the people and the excitement. And I (enjoy) 3 ...enjoy... doing a job that (be) 4 ...'s... always different.

(you write) 5 ...Do you write... your own songs?

No, I'm afraid I (not know) 6 ...don't know... how to write music. The band (look for) 7 ...'s looking for... someone to write songs at the moment.

(you / play) 8 ...Do you play... any instruments?

Well, not really, although I (learn) 9 ...'m learning... to play the piano now. The band (need) 10 ...needs... some piano music for the album we (make) 11 ...'re making... in two months' time.

(you / rehearse) 12 ...'re going... at the moment?

Oh yes, we (work) 13 ...'re working... very hard just now. We (give) 14 ...'re giving... a concert in January and we (have to) 15 ...have to... be ready.

(you / get on well) 16 ...Do you get on well... with each other?

Oh yes, we do. We (not argue) 17 ...don't argue... at all. Well, not very often!

LISTENING

3 **Listen and label the photograph with the correct names.**

Alice

Peter

Sarah

Helen

Jack

4 **Look at the photograph and listen again. In your notebook, write what each person is doing, using the present continuous tense. Then write some information about each person, using the present simple tense.**

Jack is drying himself. He is married and has a child.

SPEECHWORK: pronunciation

Present simple question forms

5 **Study the pronunciation, then listen to the tape and do the drills.**

Where do you work? / dʒuː /
Where do they live? / dəðeɪ /
What does she do? / dəzʃi /

6 **Listen and tick the sentences which you hear.**

	a) They live here.	✓	3	a) We have to stay here.	
	b) Do they live here?			b) Do we have to stay here?	✓
1	a) I know you.	✓	4	a) They all study English.	✓
	b) Do I know you?			b) Do they all study English?	
2	a) You drive this car.		5	a) You work very hard.	✓
	b) Do you drive this car?	✓		b) Do you work very hard?	

Unit 3

VOCABULARY: shopping

1 Label the items correctly, writing the main stress in capital letters.

video cassette cassette compact disc album single receipt
paperback hardback marker pen magazine writing paper

LISTENING

2 Listen and write the prices.

£5.50 1 .... 2 .... 3 .... 4 .... 5 ....

SPEECHWORK: stress and intonation

Asking for things

3 Study the stress and intonation, then listen to the tape and do the drills.

Have you got the LATest Simply RED album?

Have you got any RECords by Simply RED?

Unit 4

GRAMMAR: *not allowed to/not supposed to*

1 **Read the boarding school rules and explain them to a new pupil. Write a sentence for rules 1 to 5, using *You're not allowed to.***

1 (have) *You're not allowed to have visitors in your bedroom.*
2 (drink) ....
3 (smoke) ....
4 (put) ....
5 (have) ....

2 **Some rules are often broken. Write a sentence for rules 6 to 10, using *You're not supposed to ...., but everyone does.***

6 (talk) *You're not supposed to talk after 9.30, but everyone does.*
7 (play) ....
....
8 (eat) ....
9 (talk) ....
10 (take) ....
....

GRAMMAR: revision

3 **Match the sentences on the left with those nearest in meaning on the right.**

We're not allowed to stay. [E]
1 We're not supposed to go. [ ]
2 We don't have to go. [ ]
3 We can't go. [ ]
4 We might go. [ ]
5 Let's not go. [ ]

A We shouldn't really go.
B We're not able to go.
C Let's stay here.
D Maybe we'll go.
E We have to go.
F We can stay if we want.

Unit 5

VOCABULARY

1 **Write the words in the box under the correct dictionary definitions.**

extrovert	talent	rebel	tease	shy	conformist

n a person who [redacted] : *Anti-government* [redacted] *have seized the radio station.* | *Tom's always been a bit of a* [redacted]; *he hates conforming.* | [redacted] *tribesmen* | *a* [redacted] *stronghold*

rebel

adj, n usu. derog (of) a person who conforms to the established rules, values, and customs of society

1 ....

n **1** .a person who likes to spend time in activities with other people rather than being quiet and alone **2** *infml* a cheerful confident person

2 ....

v **1** [I;T] to make jokes about or laugh at unkindly or playfully: *At school the other children always* [redacted] *me because I was fat.* | *Don't take it seriously — he was only* [redacted]. **2** [T] to annoy (an animal or person) on purpose: *Stop* [redacted] *the cat!*

3 ....

n **1** [S (**for**);U] (a) special natural ability or skill: *He has a* [redacted] *for drawing.* | *She has great musical/artistic* [redacted]. —see GENIUS (USAGE)

4 ....

adj **1** [(**of**)] nervous in the company of others; lacking self-confidence: *When the children met the queen, they were too* [redacted] *to speak.* | *He's* [redacted] *of women.* | *a* [redacted] *smile*

5 ....

GRAMMAR: linking devices

2 **Circle the correct linking words.**

PEOPLE I LIKE TO BE FRIENDS WITH

In general, I like extrovert people <u>but/because</u> I'm rather extrovert <u>and/but</u> I like people who are similar to me. They should be good at <u>both/neither</u> talking and listening, <u>because/so</u> it's important to share ideas and experiences.

The person I like the most is extrovert and good fun <u>as well as/but also</u> being very intelligent. She's very thoughtful too. She always thinks about other people first <u>because/and</u> that's why I like her.

WRITING

3 **In your notebook, write two paragraphs about the sort of people you like to be friends with, and the person whom you like most.**

Unit 6

GRAMMAR: past simple and past continuous

1 Write the correct form of the verbs, using the past simple or past continuous tenses.

1 PAT: So how (you / meet) ...did you meet..... him then?

ANN: Well, I (work) ....was working..... in a coffee shop at the time and he often (come in) .... for his breakfast. One day, as he (leave) .... the shop, I (call out) ....: 'See you tomorrow then', and the next day we just (start) .... talking.

2 DAN: I (see) .... Joanna and Sue in the park on Saturday.

ROB: Oh yes. (they / play) .... tennis? They usually do on Saturdays.

DAN: No, they (not / be) .... They (run) .... round the park.

ROB: (You / say) .... hello?

DAN: Yes, I (shout) .... but they (not / answer) ....

ROB: Maybe they (not / see) .... you.

LISTENING: past simple and past continuous

2 Listen to the scenes and write what happened.

It was a Sunday afternoon in the park. The birds ....were singing...., children ....were playing..., and some people .....were playing tennis...... . Suddenly it ...began..... to rain, and everybody .....ran...... into the park café.

1 Mr and Mrs Williams [1] .... television when the doorbell [2] .... Mrs Williams [3] .... to answer it but when she [4] .... the door, there [5] .... no-one there.

2 It was three o'clock in the morning and Mark [1] .... Suddenly, there [2] .... a crash and he [3] .... The people next door [4] .... Then one of them [5] .... a plate across the room. The other one [6] .... and then it [7] .... quiet.

CROSSWORD

3 **Complete the crossword, using the notes which Sue Barnes wrote before she started her trip to the USA.**

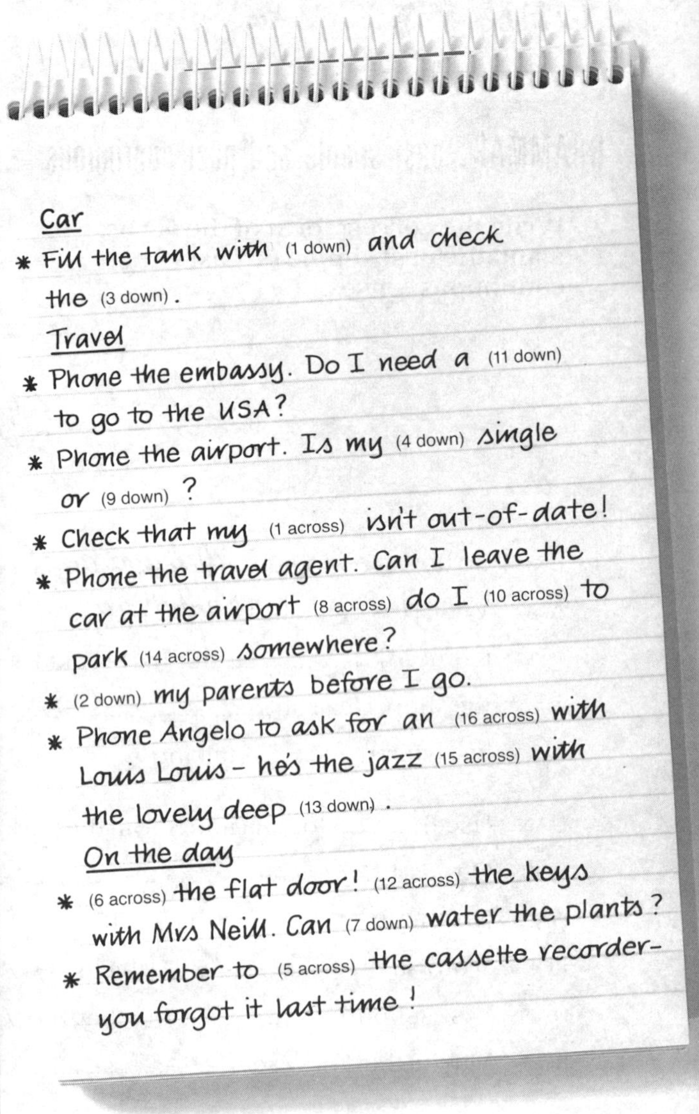

SPEECHWORK: pronunciation

Past simple question forms

4 **Study the pronunciation, then listen to the tape and do the drills.**

What did you do? / dɪdʒuː /
Where did they go? / dɪd ðeɪ /

5 **Listen and circle the word which you hear.**

(*Did*) / *Do* you like it?

1 *Did / Do* you agree?

2 *Are / Were* they waiting for you?

3 *Was / Is* she sitting outside?

4 *Did / Do* they want to stay long?

5 *Was / Is* it raining?

6 *Did / Do* you always stay there?

7 *Are / Were* they going out?

Unit 7

VOCABULARY: compound nouns

1 **Look below at the compound nouns using *house* or *home*. Tick the ones which you know. Look up the words which you don't know in a dictionary.**

housewife	....	house-warming	....	homework	....
homecoming	....	house-trained	....	homesick	....
houseproud	....	housekeeper	....	home-made	....
houseboat	....				

Now write the correct words next to the definitions below.

A place to live in (on water). ...*houseboat*..........

1 A person who's very tidy at home. ....

2 You may feel this if you're away from home for a while. ....

3 A party you give when you move to a new place. ....

4 A word to describe food (for example, bread) which you make yourself. ....

GRAMMAR: time connectors

2 **A reporter is interviewing Isabel Browning, a skater. Complete the interview using the words or phrases in the box.**

after / during / in / when / at the age of / eventually / now / at / for / at first / for a time

REPORTER: So you've been a serious skater ..*for*.... about ten years now. How old were you (1) .... you first started skating?

ISABEL: I started going to skating classes (2) .... five.

REPORTER: Five! That's very young. Were you a good skater?

ISABEL: Well, no. I didn't really enjoy it (3) .... and (4) .... I tried to refuse to go – but (5) .... winning my first competition, I decided I really liked it.

REPORTER: And when did that happen?

ISABEL: That was (6) .... 1978. After that, I practised all the time (7) .... weekends and (8) .... the school holidays. And (9) .... I was good enough to enter big competitions.

REPORTER: And (10) .... you're the south-east champion!

WRITING

3 **In your notebook, write the reporter's article about Isabel. Start like this:**

The new south-east skating champion is Isabel Browning.

Unit 8

COMMUNICATION: polite responses

1 Choose the correct polite response by circling a) or b).

	Sorry!	a) You'd better be. (b) Don't worry about it.
1	I've just passed my exams.	a) Never mind. b) Congratulations.
2	Can I borrow your pen?	a) Of course not. b) Certainly.
3	What's the time please?	a) I don't know. b) Sorry, I've no idea.
4	I'm sorry!	a) So you should be. b) It doesn't matter.
5	We're getting married.	a) That's all right. b) That's wonderful news.
6	He's in hospital.	a) Oh dear. b) Get well soon.
7	Sorry I'm late.	a) Don't worry about it. b) Don't do it again.

WRITING

2 Alan has just spilt wine over his friend Bob's jacket. Write a dialogue using the instructions below.

Alan apologises to Bob.	ALAN:	*Oh no! I'm terribly sorry, Bob!*
Bob responds to the apology.	BOB:	....
Alan asks if the jacket is washable.	ALAN:	....
Bob says that it isn't.	BOB:	....
Alan offers to pay the dry cleaning bill.	ALAN:	....
Bob refuses the offer, politely.	BOB:	....
Alan apologises again.	ALAN:	....
Bob responds to the apology.	BOB:	....

SPEECHWORK: stress and intonation

Apologies

3 Study the stress and intonation, then listen to the tape and do the drills.

SOrry. I'm SOrry. I'm TERRibly SOrry.

I'm AWfully SOrry. I REAlly AM SOrry.

4 Listen to the apologies and write which sounds more sorry, a or b.

[*a*] 1 [ ] 2 [ ] 3 [ ] 4 [ ]

Unit 9

GRAMMAR: *used to/be used to*

1 Write sentences, choosing the correct form of *used to* or *be used to*.

I (used to / am used to) go to bed at 7.30.

I used to go to bed at 7.30.

1 They (didn't use to / aren't used to) getting up early.

....

2 You (used to / are used to) be good at football, didn't you?

....

3 (Didn't she use to / Isn't she used to) have long hair?

....

4 I (didn't use to / am not used to) being out so late.

....

5 He (used to / is used to) hard work.

....

6 This (used to / is used to) be an attractive area.

....

2 Melanie is talking about her past and her life now. Complete the text with the correct form of *used to* or *(not) be used to*.

'I*'m used to*... living in the town now, but it took a long time. I hated it for years. As a child, I ....*used to*..... live in the countryside and I loved it. My friends and I [1] .... go out in the fields and play all day. It was wonderful.

When I was thirteen, we moved to the town. Nowadays, I [2] .... all the cars and the noise but it was a shock then. I [3] .... hurry home from school and hide in my bedroom.

Even after all these years, however, I [4] .... some things. People in towns are very unfriendly and towns are sometimes quite dangerous. In the country, I [5] .... go out by myself but nowadays I usually take a friend. And my parents drive me around a lot – they [6] .... getting phone calls from me, asking for a lift home!'

READING: facts about Britain

3 **Look at the chart and read the text. Then answer the questions.**

MEAT? Yuck! say kids

VEGETARIANS USED TO BE REGARDED AS VERY STRANGE IN BRITAIN but vegetarianism is now becoming much more popular. Many people who used to eat meat regularly are now avoiding it – 1.3 million adults in fact, 3 per cent of the adult population.

Children appear to be more vegetarian than their parents; 1.4 million children are either fully vegetarian or avoid red meat. Their reasons for this are given in the chart.

Altogether, 7.7 per cent of the British population are either full vegetarians or avoid red meat. There has been an 11 per cent increase in this figure over the last year.

Their reasons for more popular

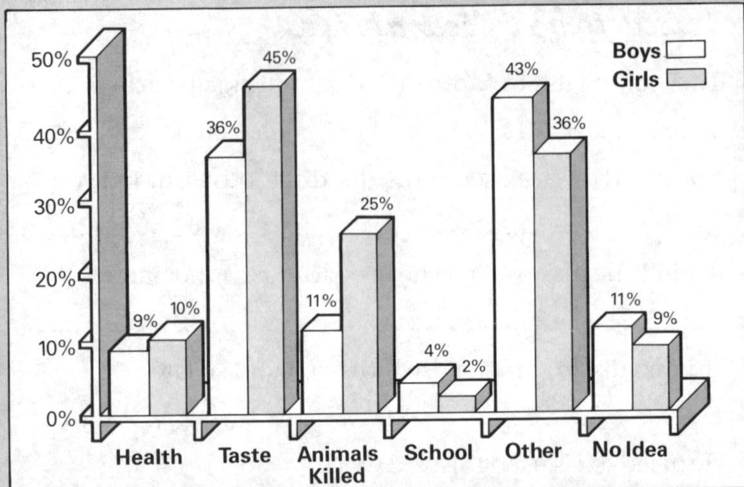

Reasons given for children not eating, or avoiding, meat in their diets

Are these statements true or false? Write T or F in the boxes.

1 There are more vegetarian adults than children in Britain. ☐

2 The number of vegetarians has increased in the last year. ☐

3 Nearly eight per cent of the British population avoids meat of some sort. ☐

4 Vegetarianism used to be more popular in Britain. ☐

5 Of all the reasons that children give for avoiding meat,
a) more than a tenth of the girls gave health as a reason. ☐
b) nearly half of the girls said it was because of the taste. ☐
c) more than a tenth of the boys had no idea of the reason. ☐
d) a quarter of the girls didn't like animals being killed. ☐
e) a tenth of the boys said it was because of the taste. ☐
f) over a third of the girls had other reasons. ☐

SPEECHWORK: pronunciation

Used to

4 **Study the pronunciation, then listen to the tape and do the drills.**

Before a consonant: I <u>used to</u> have a car. / ju:stə /

Before a vowel: I <u>used to</u> enjoy school. / ju:stʊ /

Source for chart above: Gallup Survey conducted for The Realeat Company 1987

Unit 10

PREPOSITIONS

1 These sentences or phrases are from *Cider with Rosie*. Complete them with *on* or *in*.

On .... the floor below, Mother and Tony shared one bedroom.

1 But most of the time we spent .... the kitchen.

2 We trod .... each other like birds .... a nest.

3 Coal crackled .... a black fireplace.

4 Towels hung to dry .... the fireguard.

5 There were boxes, books and papers .... every chair.

6 The windows were crowded with plants .... pots.

2 These phrases are also from *Cider with Rosie*. Insert *of* in the correct place.

there were eight of us in that cottage

1 a procession half-seen figures

2 showing the marks our boots

3 collection fine old china

4 But most the time

5 potatoes unusual shape

6 coal and sticks beech wood

7 six tables different sizes

CROSSWORD

3 Complete the crossword.

ACROSS

2 Black stone used as fuel. (4)
5 Musical instrument. (5)
6 All numbers added together. (5)
7 .... quick as you can. (2)
9 Old-fashioned type of light. (6)
10 Don't ask me – ask someone .... (4)
14 New, up-to-date. (6)
15 Not asleep. (5)
16 Type of bowl for plants. (3)

DOWN

1 Make a noise like a burning fire. (7)
2 Old, small house. (7)
3 Top floor in some houses. (5)
4 Long chair, settee. (4)
5 Flower, bush, or vegetable. (5)
8 Quiet. (6)
11 Opposite of 'high'. (3)
12 We went sleepily .... bed. (2)
13 Place where birds live. (4)
14 Give it to ...., please, it's mine. (2)

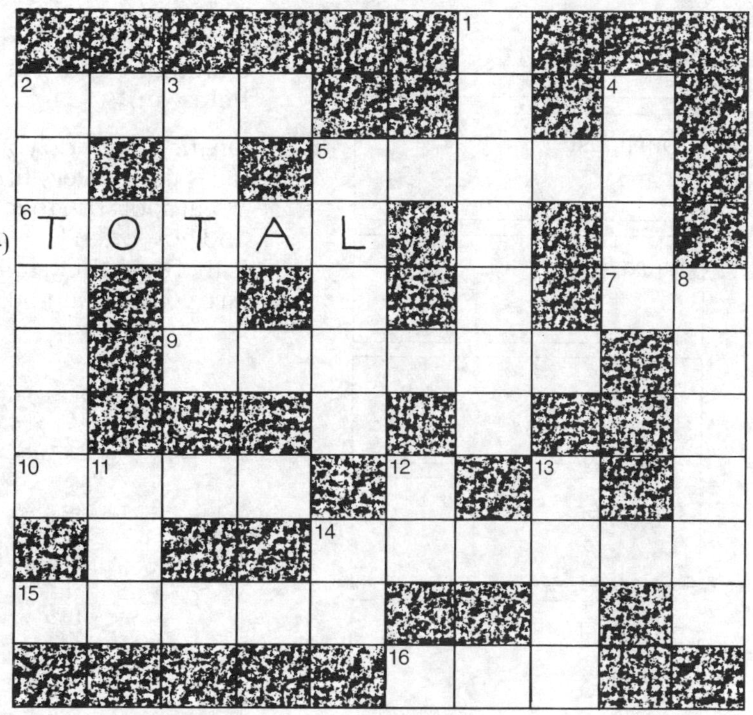

Unit 11

VOCABULARY: money

1 **Complete the letter with the correct words from the box.**

rise	cost of living
pay	paid
afford	rich
cost	money

Dear Tony,

Well, here I am in London. I've got a job now as a receptionist in a hotel but it's very badly ______. The 1 ______ here is quite high and I don't think that I can 2 ______ to stay much longer. It's very nice in London if you're 3 ______, though. Maybe I'll come back when I've got lots of 4 ______. The 5 ______ of accommodation is the worst. I 6 ______ £50 a week for one room. I'm going to ask for a 7 ______ at the hotel but I don't think they'll give me one, so I'll probably see you soon!

Best wishes,

Richard

WORD FORMATION: jobs

2 **Write the activity or subject connected with these jobs.**

- typist — *typing*
- photographer
- actor
- journalist
- hairdresser
- scientist
- engineer
- physicist

WRITING

3 **How fit are you? Read the paragraphs below, then write a similar report in your notebook. Use the questions to help you.**

1 On the whole, do you think that you're very fit / fairly fit / not very fit?
2 What sport or other form of exercise do you do, and how often?
3 Is there anything unhealthy about your lifestyle?
4 Are you as fit as you would like to be?

On the whole, I think I'm fairly fit. I nearly always walk to work, which is about a kilometre away, I play tennis most weekends and I sometimes go swimming.

I probably eat too many chips and drink too much Coke and unfortunately I spend a lot of time at work sitting at a desk.

I'd like to be really fit but I'm too lazy.

Unit 12

GRAMMAR: *Going to/will*

1 Write the correct form of *going to* or *will*.

A: Don't forget, it's Jo's birthday tomorrow.

B: Is it? O.K., I *'ll* send her a card this afternoon.

A: What are your plans for the summer?

B: We*'re going to* spend the whole summer by the sea.

1 Oh no, look at that child. She .... fall off her bike!

2 I think Ruth .... pass her exams without much difficulty.

3 Those bags look heavy. I .... carry one for you.

4 A: Now don't forget to phone us.

B: Don't worry. I .... phone every day.

5 If my grades are good, I .... get a place at university.

6 Millions of people .... die of hunger again next year.

2 Complete the table, using all the sentences from Exercise 1.

going to	1 predictions about the future from evidence in the present	*Look at that child. She's going to fall off her bike!*
	2 future plans decided before the time of speaking	
will	3 predictions about the future	*I think Ruth will pass her exams without much difficulty.*
	4 sudden decision made at the moment of speaking	
	5 promises	
	6 offers	
	7 with clauses of condition and time	
	8 statements of fact about the future	

READING

3 Read the article and answer the questions.

I'm going to have a very unusual holiday this year. I'm going to photograph elephants in Africa. If you want to do the same, you'd better book your ticket soon. There won't be any wild elephants in twenty years' time. They'll all be dead, except maybe for a few in nature reserves.

An elephant is a walking bank as far as hunters are concerned. The reason is the price of ivory, which was $5 a kilogram in the 1960s but is $50 a kilogram now. As the price went up, the killings started. Elephant populations in eastern Africa started falling and now the total African population is declining fast.

The largest estimate says that there are about 800,000 African elephants. In ten years' time, this figure will be halved if hunting continues as it is now. Another ten years, and the wild elephant will no longer exist.

Sixteen of the thirty-five African countries which have elephants are going to restrict trade in elephant products and some of these are going to start special nature reserves, where elephants are protected. But it may be too late. If the hunting continues on its present scale, the elephant will soon be a thing of the past.

Are these statements true or false? Write T or F in the boxes.

1 The writer is going on to have an ordinary holiday this year. ☐
2 The writer is going to hunt elephants. ☐
3 All the world's wild elephants will be dead in twenty years if hunting continues at its present rate. ☐
4 Elephants are hunted for their meat. ☐
5 The price of ivory has fallen since the 1960s. ☐
6 In ten years, there will be twice as many African elephants as there are now. ☐
7 The number of elephants in Africa is falling rapidly. ☐
8 Some countries are going to protect the wild elephant. ☐

SPEECHWORK: pronunciation

Going to/will

4 Study the pronunciation, then listen to the tape and do the drills.

Before a vowel: They're going to arrive on Saturday. / gəʊɪŋtʊ /

Before a consonant: They're going to come on Saturday. / gəʊɪŋtə /

5 Listen and tick the sentences which you hear.

a) I go to that school. ☐
b) I'll go to that school. ✓

1 a) You sleep in this room. ☐
b) You'll sleep in this room. ☐

2 a) She'll be here tomorrow. ☐
b) He'll be here tomorrow. ☐

3 a) They arrive at three. ☐
b) They'll arrive at three. ☐

4 a) We stay in a hotel. ☐
b) We'll stay in a hotel. ☐

5 a) They live with her parents. ☐
b) They'll live with her parents. ☐

Unit 13

COMMUNICATION: requests

1 Complete the sentences.

It's a bit dark in here. Could you *turn on the light (please)?*

1 I can't get to sleep with the music so loud. Could you ....

2 Oh, I haven't got my dictionary here. Could I ....

3 Our phone's not working. Do you think I ....

4 Excuse me, I've forgotten to post this letter. Do you think you ....

5 I'm afraid there are a lot of typing mistakes in this letter. Would you mind ....

....

6 I'm afraid your car's in the way. Would you mind ....

VOCABULARY

2 Match the words with their dictionary definitions and pronunciation.

receptionist	1	*v* **1** [I;T (**to**)] to take (goods, letters, etc.) to people's houses or places of work: *Letters are* [redacted] *every day.* | *Yes, we* [redacted] *newspapers.* | *Will you* [redacted] *, or do I have to come to the shop to collect the goods?*	A /dɪˈlɪvəʳ/
receipt	2	*n* **1** [C] a written statement that one has received money (or sometimes goods): *Ask the shop for a* [redacted] *when you pay the bill.* | *The assistant will* **make out** (= write) **a** [redacted]	B /ˈɜːdʒənt/
urgent	3	*v* [I;T] **1** to write (one's name) on (a written paper), esp. for official purposes, to show one's agreement, show that one is the writer, etc.: [redacted] *here, please.* | *The documents are ready to be* [redacted]. | *He* [redacted] *(his name on) the cheque.* | *The USSR has just* [redacted] *a new trade agreement with Japan.* (= reached an agreement and made it formally complete by [redacted] a paper)	C /saɪn/
deliver	4	*n* a person who welcomes or deals with people arriving in a hotel or place of business, visiting a doctor, etc.	D /rɪˈsiːt/
sign	5	*adj* **1** very important and needing to be dealt with quickly or first: *It's not* [redacted]*; it can wait until tomorrow.* | *a very* [redacted] *message* | *in* [redacted] *need of medical attention*	E /rɪˈsepʃənɪ̈st/

SPEECHWORK: stress and intonation

Asking people to do things

3 Study the stress and intonation, then listen to the tape and do the drills.

Could you TAKE this to the comPUter centre, PLEASE?

Do you think you could HURRy?

Would you mind asking them to CALL me?

Unit 14

GRAMMAR: *can/could/be able to*

1 Complete the sentences, using the correct form of *can, could* or *be able to*. If two answers are possible, choose one.

She ...can... understand quite a lot of English but she ...can't... speak it.

1 I don't think I .... go on holiday this year, I .... afford it.

2 I .... find my way anywhere when I first came to this town.

3 My last job was near my home, so I .... walk to work.

4 I hope to .... work abroad when I leave university.

5 I .... phone you last night because our phone wasn't working.

6 My girlfriend bought a car last year so we .... go out a lot more since then.

2 Complete the text, using *could (not)* or the correct form of *be able to*. If two answers are possible, choose one.

Jane ...could... swim when she was a baby. Her parents lived next door to a swimming pool so they ...were able to... take her swimming every day. By the time she was five, she [1] .... swim twenty lengths of the pool.

When she started school, it was no longer possible to go to the pool each day but she went as often as she [2] .... Soon, she started entering competitions and she [3] .... win them all without any difficulty. She wanted to have a swimming coach but her parents [4] .... (not) afford to pay for one.

However, she won the National Junior Championship when she was only thirteen. Her teachers think that next year she [5] .... win the Senior Championship, too, if she has a good coach.

SPEECHWORK: pronunciation

Can/can't

3 Study the pronunciation, then listen to the tape and do the drills.

She can sing very well. / kən /

She can't read music. / kɑːnt /

Yes, I can. / kæn /

Unit 15

VOCABULARY: adjectives

1 Complete the adjectives below. They all have pleasant associations.

b e a u t i f u l   3 s p _ c _ _ _ _ l _ _

1 w _ n _ _ _ f _ _   4 m _ g _ _ _ _ _ c _ _ _

2 d _ l _ _ _ _ _ _ s   5 f _ _ t _ _ t _ c

2 Complete the adjectives below. They have unpleasant associations.

1 t _ _ r _ _ _ _ e   2 d _ _ _ d _ _ _ l   3 a _ f _ l

WORD FORMATION

3 Write the adjectives in their negative form by adding *un-, in-. im-,* or *ir-*. Use your dictionary if you wish.

possible complete comfortable regular correct
happy polite expensive able perfect clear
patient formal probable forgettable responsible

un-	in-	im-	ir-
uncomfortable	incomplete	impossible	irregular

PREPOSITIONS: position and movement

4 Circle the correct prepositions.

'We start our tour (at)/*on* Camden Lock Market, where you will have time to browse 1 *across/among* the stalls. A riverboat will then take you 2 *in/on* a gentle cruise 3 *along/through* Regent's Park Canal 4 *along/through* the beautiful surroundings of Regent's Park and London Zoo. Lunch will be served 5 *at/on* board. We then make our way 6 *among/across* London 7 *to/at* the South Bank. 8 *Across/From* there our route takes us 9 *along/on* the Embankment 10 *past/across* the magnificent new Chelsea Wharf development.'

Unit 16

GRAMMAR: the first conditional

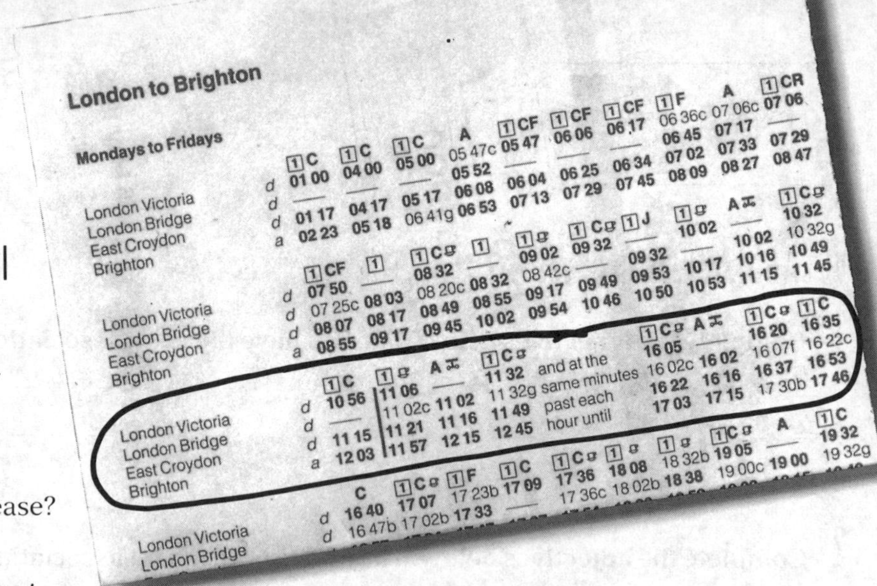

London to Brighton

Mondays to Fridays

		[1] C	[1] C	[1] C	A	[1] CF	[1] CF	[1] CF	[1] F	A	[1] CR
London Victoria	d	01 00	04 00	05 00	05 47c	05 47	06 06	06 17	06 36c	07 06c	07 06
London Bridge	d	—	—	—	05 52	—	—	—	06 45	07 17	—
East Croydon	d	01 17	04 17	05 17	06 08	06 04	06 25	06 34	07 02	07 33	07 29
Brighton	a	02 23	05 18	06 41g	06 53	07 13	07 29	07 45	08 09	08 27	08 47

		[1] CF	[1]	[1] C	[1]	[1]	[1] C	[1] J	[1]	A	[1] C
London Victoria	d	07 50	—	08 32	—	09 02	09 32	—	10 02	—	10 32
London Bridge	d	07 25c	08 03	08 20c	08 32	08 42c	—	09 32	—	10 02	10 32g
East Croydon	d	08 07	08 17	08 49	08 55	09 17	09 49	09 53	10 17	10 16	10 49
Brighton	a	08 55	09 17	09 45	10 02	09 54	10 46	10 50	10 53	11 15	11 45

		[1] C	[1]	A	[1] C		[1] C	A	[1] C	[1] C
London Victoria	d	10 56	11 06	—	11 32	and at the	16 05	—	16 20	16 35
London Bridge	d	—	11 02c	11 02	11 32g	same minutes	16 02c	16 02	16 07f	16 22c
East Croydon	d	11 15	11 21	11 16	11 49	past each	16 22	16 16	16 37	16 53
Brighton	a	12 03	11 57	12 15	12 45	hour until	17 03	17 15	17 30b	17 46

		C	[1] C	[1] F	[1] C	[1] C	[1]	[1]	[1] C	A	[1] C
London Victoria	d	16 40	17 07	17 23b	17 09	17 36	18 08	18 32b	19 05	—	19 32
London Bridge	d	16 47b	17 02b	17 33	—	17 36c	18 02b	18 38	19 00c	19 00	19 32g

1 Look at the timetable and complete the conversation, using the first conditional.

PASSENGER: Could you tell me how long it takes to get to Brighton, please?

CLERK: Well, if you *catch* a fast train, it *'ll take* fifty-one minutes.

If you [1] .... a slow train, it [2] .... an hour and thirteen minutes.

PASSENGER: I see. Well I'd like to arrive in Brighton before twelve o'clock if possible.

CLERK: Well, the next train is at 11.06. If you [3] .... that one, you [4] .... at 11.57.

PASSENGER: And if I miss it?

CLERK: If you [5] .... it, you .... have to [6] .... the 11.32, and that gets in at quarter to one.

PASSENGER: O.K. Thanks. I'll have a return to Brighton then, please.

CLERK: Here you are. That's £14.80. It's five to eleven now, so if you hurry, you [7] .... the 11.06.

2 Melanie is going on holiday with a friend but her parents are worried. Complete their questions.

What'll you do if you miss .... the boat?

We'll catch the next one, of course.

1 .... anywhere to stay?

Oh, don't worry, we'll find somewhere. There are lots of hotels.

2 .... your money?

I'll phone you and ask you to send me some more.

3 .... ill?

I'll go and see a doctor.

4 .... lost?

We won't get lost. I've got maps of the whole area.

READING

3 **Match the extracts about transport in London with the systems of transport below.**

A These are reasonable in price, the drivers always know the fastest routes and you'll have a very comfortable journey.

B This is a very efficient way of getting around London. You won't see much of the city but you will get to your destination quickly. There are nearly 300 stations, so you'll usually find one close by.

C For people with time and energy, this is the best way of travelling short distances. You'll be able to stop and look at anything that interests you and it'll give you a sense of the 'atmosphere' of London.

D The traffic is sometimes slow but you'll get a good view of the city, especially if you sit on the top deck.

E This is one of the fastest ways of travelling across central London but you'll have to be careful. You can hire one from the firms listed here.

F Traffic congestion in central London is a problem, so your journey will probably be very slow, and parking can be difficult.

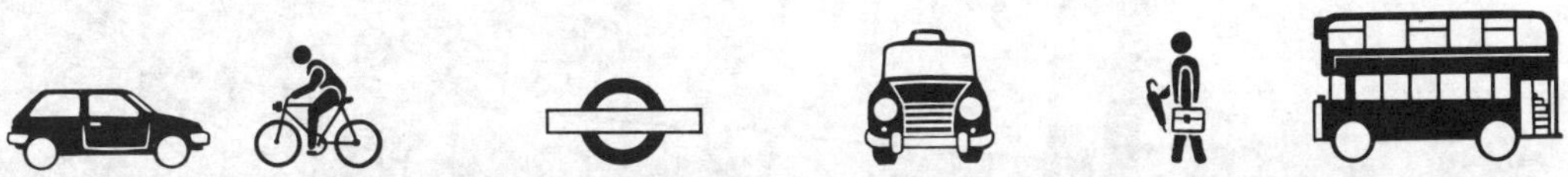

car [F] 1 bike [ ] 2 underground [ ] 3 taxi [ ] 4 walking [ ] 5 bus [ ]

WRITING

4 **Use the information in Exercise 3 to write advice about the systems of transport in London.**

car *If you go by car, your journey will probably be very slow.*

1 bike ....

2 underground ....

3 taxi ....

4 walking ....

5 bus ....

Unit 17

VOCABULARY

1 **Find eight more sports in lines across the wordsquare, and five more places to play sport in lines going down it. Write them below.**

SPORTS

football ....

....

....

....

....

....

....

....

....

PLACES

track ....

....

....

....

....

....

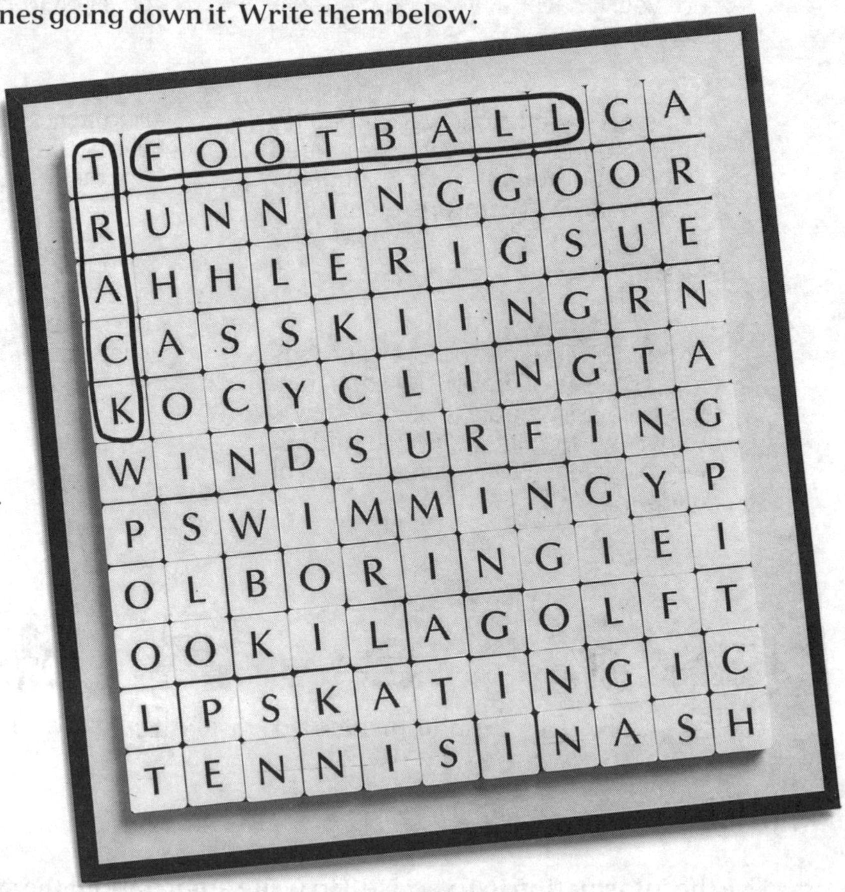

2 **Look at these different ways of describing sport.**

play + game – play football / tennis
go + *-ing* – go swimming / running
go for a + noun – go for a swim / a walk

Using some of the sports in Exercise 1, write five sentences about a person who does a different sport every day.

She plays tennis on Saturdays. ....

1 ....

2 ....

3 ....

4 ....

5 ....

LISTENING

3 **Listen to the holiday advertisements and complete the table.**

Place	Number of sports	Types of sports
The Gambia	*5*	*windsurfing, waterskiing, swimming, tennis, golf*

Which place(s) would you like to go to and why?

I'd like to go to .... *because* ....

....

....

....

WRITING

4 **Read the extract from a holiday brochure, then, in your notebook, write a similar paragraph about sports facilities in an area of your country. You can use the expressions in the box if you wish.**

... offers ...... facilities ...

If you enjoy ......, you'll find ...

There are many ...... available ...

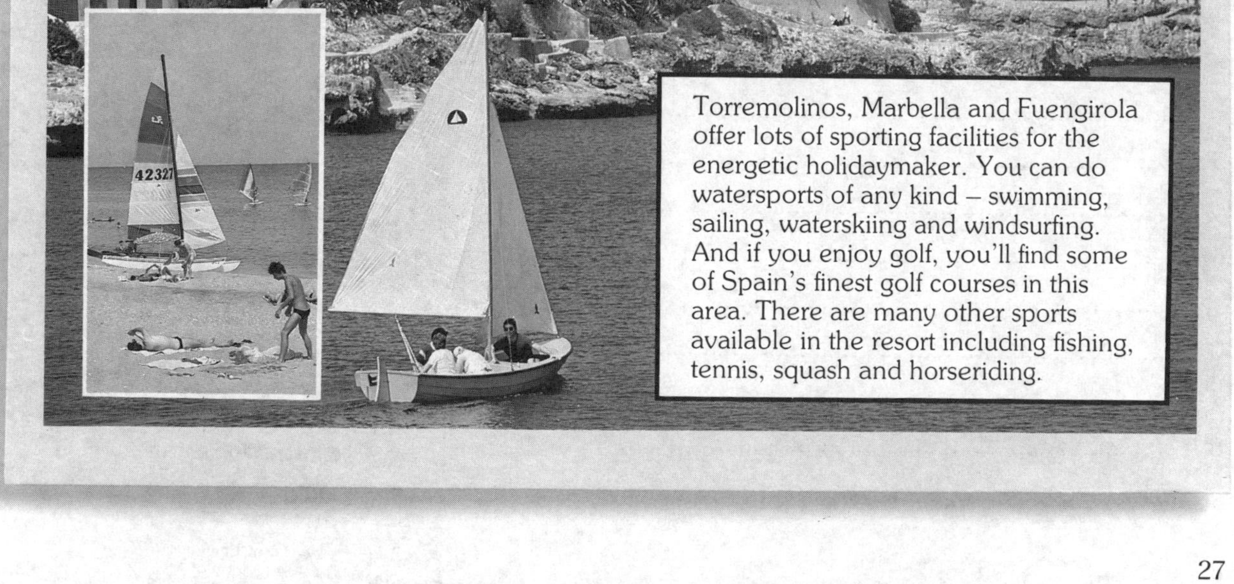

Torremolinos, Marbella and Fuengirola offer lots of sporting facilities for the energetic holidaymaker. You can do watersports of any kind – swimming, sailing, waterskiing and windsurfing. And if you enjoy golf, you'll find some of Spain's finest golf courses in this area. There are many other sports available in the resort including fishing, tennis, squash and horseriding.

Unit 18

COMMUNICATION: checking information

1 Write the question tags.

You live in Birmingham, *don't you?*

1 She comes from Italy, ...

2 I've met you before, ...

3 You left school last year, ...

4 They're going to get married soon, ...

5 You'll be twenty next birthday, ...

6 You used to have a car like that, ...

7 He's supposed to be at work, ...

2 Rewrite the sentences in Exercise 1 as negative questions.

Don't you live in Birmingham?

1 ....

2 ....

3 ....

4 ....

5 ....

6 ....

7 ....

3 A clerk is checking a journalist's work permit application in the Australian immigration office. Using the passport and business card, write eight questions using question tags.

Your name's John Thornbury, isn't it?

1 ....

2 ....

3 ....

4 ....

5 ....

6 ....

7 ....

8 ....

VOCABULARY: opposites

4 **Find the words which are opposite, or nearly opposite.**

A		B
lazy	lazy / energetic	take off
shallow	.... /	short
offer	.... /	complicated
sunny	.... /	deep
put on	.... /	energetic
lengthy	.... /	cloudy
simple	.... /	refuse

GRAMMAR: revision

5 **Circle the correct answers.**

I *go* / *am going* to the cinema quite often.

1 I'm sorry I *didn't speak* / *wasn't speaking* to you last night. I *put* / *was putting* the children to bed when the phone *rang* / *was ringing*.

2 A: Have you decided? *Are you going to come* / *Will you come* to my party on Saturday?

B: I don't think I can because my aunt and uncle *are staying* / *will stay* with us this weekend.

A: Oh, please come.

B: O.K. Well, *I'm going to try* / *I'll try* to come for a short time.

3 It was a terrible fire but eventually the firefighters *could* / *were able to* get everyone out of the building.

4 When she first *was coming* / *came* to England, she *used to* / *was used to* look the wrong way when she crossed the road, but she *used to* / *is used to* the traffic now.

5 If you *come* / *will come* tonight, I'm sure you *have* / *'ll have* a good time.

6 He *heard* / *was hearing* a shout, *jumped* / *was jumping* over the wall and *was running* / *ran* towards the house.

SPEECHWORK: stress and intonation

Checking information

6 **Study the stress and intonation, then listen to the tape and do the drills.**

ISn't there a POOL in Lansbury PARK?

THIS bus goes there, DOESn't it?

Unit 19

GRAMMAR: *in case/if/unless/when/as soon as*

1 Join the sentences, using *in case*.

Can I have a 50p piece? I might need one for the parking meter.
Can I have a 50p piece in case I need one for the parking meter?

1 Why don't you take some sandwiches? There might not be a buffet car on the train.

....

2 Take this map. You might get lost.

....

3 I'll take my sunglasses. It might be sunny.

....

4 You should always phone before you come round. I might not be in.

....

5 I always use my alarm clock. I might not wake up.

....

6 I'll stay at home. Pat might call.

....

7 We'll have to take out insurance. We might have an accident.

....

2 Match a clause from A with one from B, then write sentences using *if, unless, when, in case,* or *as soon as* using each one once.

	A		B
	Will you give her this message →	A	she works hard
1	Phone me	B	they give me a rise
2	We'd better be quiet	C	you arrive
3	I'll phone you	D	you see her
4	She should pass the exam	E	we wake the baby
5	I'll leave this job	F	I get my results

Will you give her this message if/when/as soon as you see her?

1 ....

2 ....

3 ....

4 ....

5 ....

Unit 20

LISTENING

1 **Listen to the commentary of a race for charity and complete the chart. The names of the charities are given below.**

	**Old People's Home**
	**Children's Hospital**
	**Hostel for the Homeless**
	**Animal Rescue Society**

Name	Clare Andrews	Tim Hunter	Alec Jones	John Stevens
Town				
Charity				
Position				

VOCABULARY: word formation

> Adverbs of manner are usually formed by adding *ly* to an adjective: *silent +ly =silently*. However, not all words ending in *ly* are adverbs. Some are adjectives.

2 **Write *adv* (adverb) or *adj* (adjective) above the adverbs or adjectives below.**

adj silly	adv carefully	badly	likely	hilly
perfectly	noisily	lovingly	unhappily	
lovely	lively	slowly	jolly	
beautifully	friendly	excitedly	lonely	

Unit 21

LISTENING

1 **Read the hotel menu. Listen to Glenn's conversation with the hotel customers. Find the mistakes in Glenn's order and rewrite it correctly.**

THE STRATFORD HOTEL

BREAKFAST MENU

Chilled fruit juice
Grapefruit segments
Cereals

Egg, bacon and tomato
Kippers
Scrambled egg on toast
Creamed mushroom on toast
Continental breakfast
(croissants, rolls, butter and jam)

Toast with a selection of
jams and marmalade

Tea or coffee

Table ......

Table ..5..

1 orange juice
1 cereal - cornflakes
2 mushrooms on toast
toast
1 tea
1 coffee

Glenn

VOCABULARY: *get*

2 **Answer the questions using *get* and a word from the box.**

worried	excited	dark	accepted
fired	better	old	lost	invited

Why didn't you go to Alan's party? *I didn't get invited.*

1 Why have you turned the lights on? *It's* ....
2 Are the children looking forward to their holiday? *Yes, they're* ....
3 Is Jane feeling confident about her exams? *No, she's* ....
4 The TV doesn't work very well now, does it? *No, it's* ....
5 Did you apply for that job? *Yes, and I* ....
6 I'm sorry to hear you're not very well. *That's O.K. I'm* ....
7 Why isn't James at work? *He* ....
8 Why have you bought a map? *In case I* ....

Unit 22

GRAMMAR: verb tenses

1 Put a tick (✓) by the correct sentence, and a cross (✗) by the wrong one.

a) I've been writing two letters. ☒
b) I've written two letters. ✓

1 a) I've been reading that book twice. ☐
b) I've read that book twice. ☐

2 a) I saw Jane last night. ☐
b) I've seen Jane last night. ☐

3 (It's 11 o'clock in the morning.)
a) She phoned me twice this morning. ☐
b) She's phoned me twice this morning. ☐

4 a) I've been learning English for four years now. ☐
b) I learnt English for four years now. ☐

5 a) How many times have you been out this week? ☐
b) How many times have you been going out this week? ☐

6 a) I've been reading this morning. ☐
b) I've read this morning. ☐

7 a) Where have you bought those trousers? ☐
b) Where did you buy those trousers? ☐

8 a) She hasn't done her exams yet. ☐
b) She hasn't been doing her exams yet. ☐

9 a) Did you already see that film? ☐
b) Have you already seen that film? ☐

10 a) You've been crying. What's the matter? ☐
b) You've cried. What's the matter? ☐

2 Look at the notes used by Glenn's manager when he interviewed Glenn for his job. Write complete questions, using the notes.

How long have you been in England?

1 ....
....

2 ....
....

3 ....
....

4 ....
....

5 ....
....

6 ....
....

7 ....

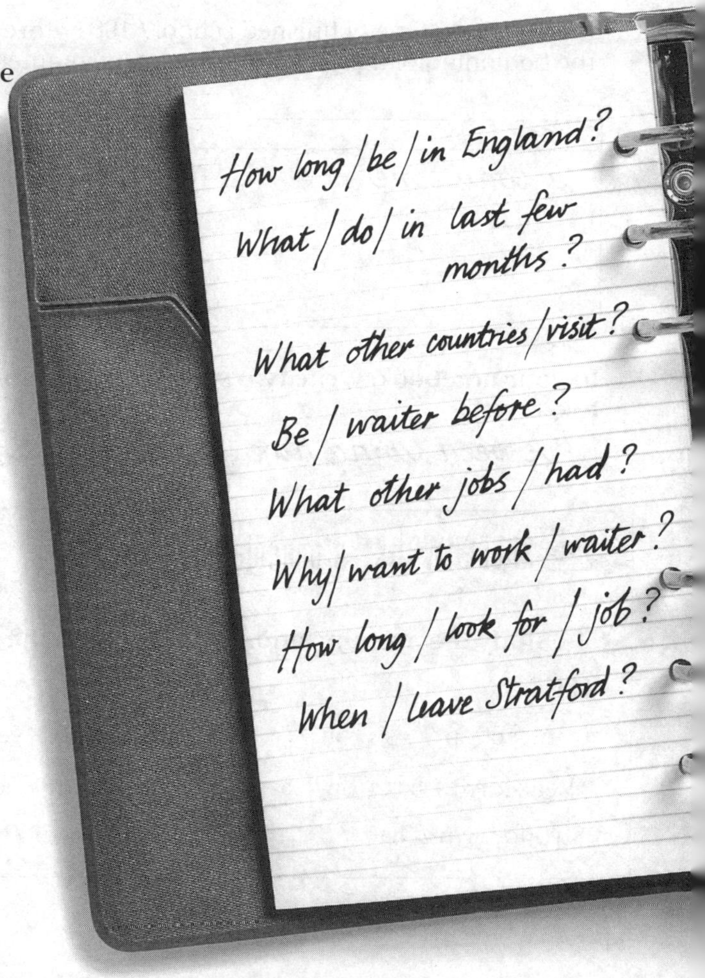

VOCABULARY: *just/yet/already*

3 Rewrite the sentences in the correct order.

to / have / shops / been / I / just / the /.

I have just been to the shops.

1 written / hasn't / yet / me / She / to /.

....

2 the / have / all / They / washing-up / done / already /.

....

3 seen / you / yet / that / Have / film / ?

....

4 good / just / me / Sarah / told / has / news / the /.

....

5 already / programme / Haven't / seen / this / we / ?

....

VOCABULARY: *for/since*

4 Write the words in the correct box.

April / a long time / I finished school / 1984 / three months / 3rd August / a week / ten years / the beginning of the year / a term / a few minutes / 9 o'clock / an hour and a half / I was a child

for	since
a long time	*April*

In your notebook, write two sentences with *for* and two with *since*, using words from the two boxes.

I've been living here for a long time.

SPEECHWORK: pronunciation

Present perfect

5 Study the pronunciation, then listen to the tape and do the drills.

Has	Have
Contraction *'s* = / s / or / z /	Contraction *'ve* = / v /
Weak form / həz / or / əz /	Weak form / həv / or / əv /
Strong form / hæz /	Strong form / hæv /

Unit 23

GRAMMAR: *is* or *has*

1 Is the *'s* in the following sentences a contraction of *is* or *has*? Write the correct full form after the sentence.

What's she been doing? ......has......

1 It's a difficult language. ....
2 Alison's working just now. ....
3 Jane's phoned three times. ....
4 How's the baby been? ....
5 He's doing his homework. ....
6 He's fallen down again. ....
7 It's finishing now. ....
8 She's been working. ....

COMMUNICATION: making complaints

2 Complete the sentences using the phrases in the box below.

is underdone	is salty	is very dark
has shrunk	has broken	doesn't work

My room ......is very dark.......

1 This soup ....
2 This meat ....
3 This zip ....
4 The coffee machine ....
5 This shirt ....

3 Now write sentences to complain about the above and to request action.

(give me a different room) I'm afraid my room is very dark. Would you mind giving me a different room?

1 (take it back to the kitchen) ....
2 (grill it for a bit longer) ....
3 (put in a new one) ....
4 (give me my money back) ....
5 (change it for a different one) ....

VOCABULARY: word formation

4 **In each line, circle the adjective which is not formed from a noun.**

	healthy	tasty	(heavy)	cloudy
1	happy	smelly	sunny	smoky
2	fruity	muddy	milky	naughty
3	hungry	leafy	pretty	meaty
4	dirty	hairy	angry	silly
5	speedy	ugly	easy	rainy

WRITING

5 **Ann bought some trousers last week. When she washed them, they shrank and the button came off. Write the dialogue between Ann and the shop assistant. Follow the instructions.**

SHOP ASSISTANT	ANN
offers assistance →	explains the problem
apologises ← →	asks for a refund
says the shop does not give refunds ← →	says she thinks the shop should give refunds
apologises again about the trousers and offers to change them ← →	refuses the offer and asks to see the manager

ASSISTANT: *Can I help you?*

ANN: ....

....

ASSISTANT: ....

ANN: ....

ASSISTANT: ....

ANN: ....

ASSISTANT: ....

ANN: ....

SPEECHWORK: stress and intonation

Making complaints and requesting action

6 **Study the stress and intonation, then listen to the tape and do the drills.**

I'm aFRAID I can't EAT this STEAK. Could you CHANGE it, PLEASE?

Unit 24

GRAMMAR: *make* or *do*

1 **Are the following words used with *make* or *do*? Write them in the correct box.**

exam	money	cake	washing-up
homework	friends	hair	noise
repairs	meal	mistake	shopping
bed	course	cleaning	arrangement

make	do
money	*an exam*

2 **Look at Andrew's list of things to do. Write sentences starting with *I've got to*.**

I've got to do my homework.

1 ....

2 ....

3 ....

4 ....

5 ....

WORD GAME

3 **Change one letter each time to make a new word.**

like	hope	big	work
lake			
late			
hate	told	car	food

Unit 25

VOCABULARY: the theatre

1 Match the items in the diagram with the words below.

spotlights ...*a*...

1 stalls ....
2 box ....
3 stage ....
4 footlights ....
5 circle ....
6 curtain ....
7 orchestra pit ....
8 balcony ....

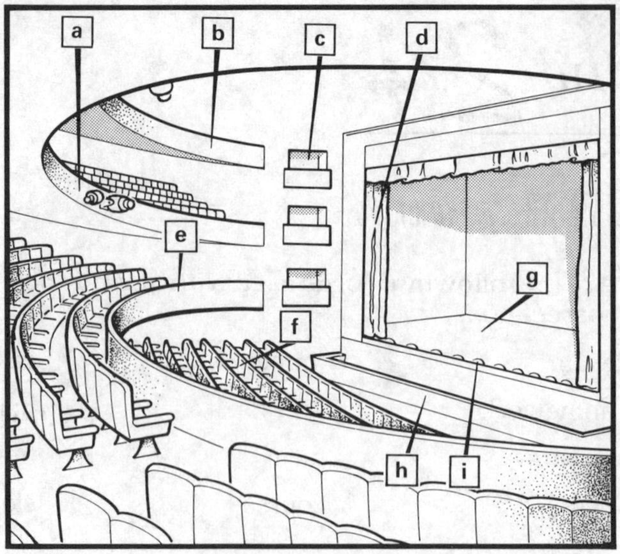

READING

2 Tick your answers to the questionnaire.

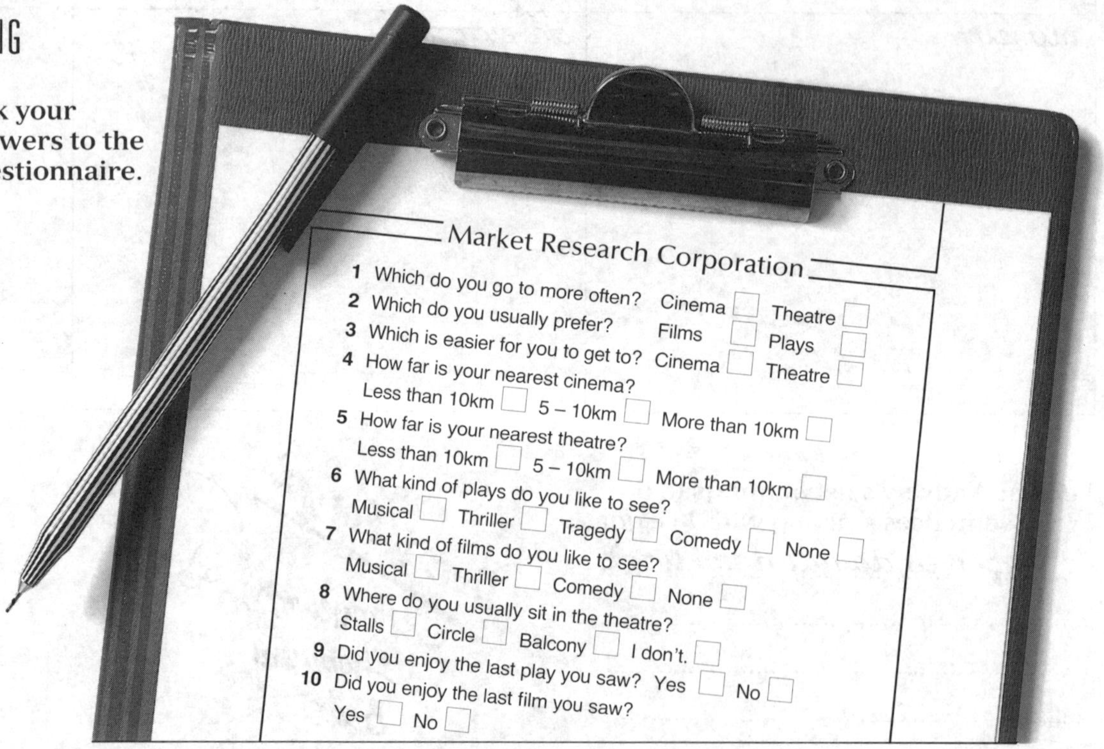

Market Research Corporation

1 Which do you go to more often? Cinema ☐ Theatre ☐
2 Which do you usually prefer? Films ☐ Plays ☐
3 Which is easier for you to get to? Cinema ☐ Theatre ☐
4 How far is your nearest cinema?
Less than 10km ☐ 5 – 10km ☐ More than 10km ☐
5 How far is your nearest theatre?
Less than 10km ☐ 5 – 10km ☐ More than 10km ☐
6 What kind of plays do you like to see?
Musical ☐ Thriller ☐ Tragedy ☐ Comedy ☐ None ☐
7 What kind of films do you like to see?
Musical ☐ Thriller ☐ Comedy ☐ None ☐
8 Where do you usually sit in the theatre?
Stalls ☐ Circle ☐ Balcony ☐ I don't. ☐
9 Did you enjoy the last play you saw? Yes ☐ No ☐
10 Did you enjoy the last film you saw?
Yes ☐ No ☐

WRITING

3 Use your answers to Exercise 2 to write two paragraphs like the ones below in your notebook. Try to connect your ideas with words like *and, but, because, so* and *also*.

I go to the cinema more often than the theatre because I generally prefer films to plays. Also, it's much easier for me to get to the cinema. The nearest cinema is only five kilometres away but the nearest theatre is about twenty.

When I go to the theatre, I like comedies. I'm not keen on tragedies or musicals. I think the best seats are in the stalls, because they're near the actors. I saw a play last week called 'Noisy Neighbours' but I didn't like it very much. It was a comedy but it wasn't very funny.

6 1 rectangle 2 square 3 cube 4 diamond 5 circle 6 triangle 7 oval

UNIT 28

2 **Example sentences:**
You're not supposed to take off your coat or sit down without being asked.
You're not supposed to ask for a drink.
You're supposed to wait until everyone is served before you start to eat./You're not supposed to start first.
You shouldn't ask for more.
You're not supposed to pour yourself a drink.
You're expected to ask if you can smoke.
You're not supposed to get up during the meal.
You're expected to stay until the end of the meal.

UNIT 29

1 1 – 2 where 3 whose 4 which 5 – (who) 6 which 7 – (which)
2 1 S 2 O 3 O 4 S 5 O 6 S
3 This is the shop I described to you.
This is the friend I knew as a child.
This is the house we're going to buy.

UNIT 30

1 ACROSS: 1 published 7 too 8 refreshing 10 who 11 reporter 13 pie 14 ever 15 industries 17 ours 19 ear 20 violin 22 as 23 ice 24 on 26 low 29 eighteen 30 fear
DOWN: 2 before 3 inexpensive 4 dance 5 at 6 colourless 9 horror movie 12 reason 16 during 18 ran 21 ill 24 owe 25 me 27 of 28 or

UNIT 31

1 1 ambitious ambition 2 flexible flexibility 3 creative creativity 4 energetic energy 5 patient patience 6 tactful tact (or tactfulness) 7 disciplined discipline 8 outgoing 9 hard-working
2 **Example adjectives:**
1 flexible 2 efficient 3 energetic 4 creative 5 hard-working 6 outgoing 7 tactful 8 ambitious
3 **Example sentences:**
1 A police officer has to be flexible, and energy is also important.
2 A secretary has to be efficient, and tact is also important.
3 A rock musician has to be energetic, and creativity is also important.
4 A writer has to be creative, and discipline is also important.
5 A nurse has to be hard-working, and patience is also important.
4 2 nurse 3 writer 4 politician

UNIT 32

1 1 had. . . would apply 2 would you do. . . saw 3 would help. . . had 4 were. . . would change 5 had. . . would you live 6 would go. . . was/were 7 would be. . . had 8 would go out. . . weren't/wasn't 9 would do. . . worked 10 wouldn't marry. . . didn't love
2 **Example sentences**
1 If I were the Prime Minister, I'd build more houses.
2 If I pass my exams, I'll have a party.
3 If I have time this weekend, I'll write some letters.
4 If I owned a yacht, I'd sail round the world.
5 If I spoke English fluently, I'd get a job as an interpreter.
6 If it rains next Saturday, I'll go to the cinema.
3 1 443 kg 2 63 kg 3 Three years 4 Thirty-two sausages, half a kilo of bacon, twelve eggs, a loaf of bread and a pot of jam 5 Fruit and nuts 6 Lying in bed
4 **Example sentences:**
If I were you, I'd take more exercise.
If I were you, I'd find some new interests.
If I were you, I'd give myself a target each week.
If I were you, I wouldn't eat any more chips.
6 1 will 2 would 3 would 4 will 5 will

UNIT 33

1 1 Could you tell me/Do you know if it's possible to take the Cambridge First Certificate exam, (please)?
2 Could you tell me/Do you know how many classes there are altogether, (please)?
3 Could you tell me/Do you know how many students there are in each class, (please)?
4 Could you tell me/Do you know if it is possible to study in the afternoons, (please)?
5 Could you tell me/Do you know what time the morning classes start, (please)?
3 1 a 2 b 3 b 4 a

UNIT 34

1 check – tyres
install – telephone
cut – hair
repair – television, telephone, car
service – car
decorate – flat
alter – dress, jacket
2 **Example sentences:**
1 I'm going to have my tyres checked.
2 I'm going to get a telephone installed.
3 I'm going to have my hair cut.
4 I'm going to get the television repaired.
5 I'm going to have my car serviced.
6 I'm going to have the flat decorated.
7 I'm going to get this dress altered.
3 1 garden 2 plain 3 clouds 4 apple 5 eggs

UNIT 35

1 disgusting, brilliant, fantastic, impossible, awful, terrific, essential, terrible
2 **Ellen's mother:** cleaning, washing-up, shopping, decorating, packing, looking after children
Ellen's father: gardening, car washing, car maintenance, decorating, packing
3 **Example questions:**
1 Who would you live with if your parents got divorced?
2 What would your parents say/do if you got home at three o'clock in the morning?
3 What would you do if some people tried to rob you?
4 What would you do if there was a fire in your house?

UNIT 36

1 1 They shouldn't have/oughtn't to have drunk all the milk.
2 She should have/ought to have worked harder.
3 We shouldn t have/oughtn't to have spent all the money yesterday.
4 They shouldn't have been/oughtn't to have been smoking in the classroom.
5 He shouldn't have been/oughtn't to have been lying in bed at 11.00.
6 I should have been/ought to have been working (when the boss came into the office).
2 1 glasses 2 attendant 3 immediately 4 stereo 5 foolish 6 plaster
3 **Example sentences:**
She should have worn a skirt and blouse./She shouldn't have worn jeans.
She shouldn't have tried to cycle to the interview./She should have taken a bus.
She shouldn't have been eating crisps when the manager came in.
She should have thought about what to say before the interview.
She should have listened more carefully to the manager's questions.
She shouldn't have asked only about the pay and the holidays.
5 1 b 2 a 3 b 4 b 5 a

UNIT 37

1 1 don't live 2 got 3 are you doing 4 'm/am visiting 5 'm/am going (to go) 6 's/is 7 Have you ever been 8 haven't 9 've/have often heard 10 lived 11 was 12 are you going to stay/staying 13 don't know 14 think 15 'll/will be 16 'll/will come
2 1 D 2 E 3 A 4 C
3 1 E 2 F 3 A 4 B 5 G 6 C
4 1 I'm feeling really tired today so I must go to bed early tonight.
2 They've got very little money. However, they seem very happy
3 I didn't like Sue when I first met her. However, I really like her now.
4 I can't do any shopping today because I've spent all my money.
5 Jerry's failed his exams so he'll have to take them again.

UNIT 38

1 1 At the London Club, Xenon. 2 She's a bouncer. 3 She asks people to keep calm. 4 No, only very occasionally. 5 (She uses) Wing Chun.
2 1 I don't know whether to look aggressive or not.
2 I don't know what to say to anyone who's arguing.
3 I don't know whether to talk to people or not.
4 I don't know what to do if there's a fight.
5 I don't know whether to use force or not.

UNIT 39

1 1 She can't have seen you.
2 She might/could have left it at home.
3 You must have met Helen before.
4 They must have been watching us.
5 They might/could have been sitting in the garden.
6 She can't have been working all night.
2 **Example sentences:**
He must have had some bad news.
He might have failed his exams.
The letter might be from his girlfriend.
His girlfriend might have decided to leave him.
4 1 F 2 T 3 T 4 F 5 F 6 T 7 T 8 F
5 1 must have 2 must have. . . can't have 3 can't have 4 could/might have 5 could/might have

UNIT 40

1 ripe, sour, sweet, juicy *orange*
mild, ripe, hard, salty, strong *cheese*
tender, fatty, lean, tough *meat*
oily, salty *fish*
mild, spicy, strong, hot *curry*
2 **At:** bedtime, 9 o'clock, the beginning of the lesson
In: August, 1988, the morning, the 1930s, the twentieth century
On: Friday, my first day at school, New Year's Day, your birthday
3 1 to 2 ago 3 to 4 for 5 When 6 ever 7 so
8 in 9 to 10 to 11 until 12 of 13 by 14 takes
15 of 16 but 17 used 18 getting 19 makes 20 of

UNIT 41

1 1 A 2 G 3 F 4 C 5 D 6 E

UNIT 42

1 1 She told me (that) they had spent a week there.
2 She told me (that) they were going to the same place next year.
3 She asked me if I/we had ever thought of going there.
4 I told her (that) we might go there one day.
5 She said (that) I/we could join them the following year.
2 1 They asked me why I was so late.
2 They asked me how I had got home.
3 They asked me what I had been doing.
4 They asked me if I had been out with you again.
5 They asked me when I was going to do my homework.
6 They asked me if I was staying in tonight.
3 1 It's for a summer camp. 2 You have English lessons.
3 You can swim at the beach, 100 metres away. 4 It's ten minutes' walk.
4 **Example sentences:**
The brochure said that the beach was only 100 metres away but it was at least a kilometre away.
The brochure said that the beach was sandy but it was stony.
The brochure said that the teachers were all native speakers of English but my teacher was Italian.
The brochure said that a wide range of activities was arranged but there was nothing arranged.
The brochure said that the town was full of things to do but there was nothing to do.
The brochure said that the town was ten minutes' walk from the camp but it was half an hour away.

UNIT 43

1 2 B 3 D 4 H 5 A 6 E 7 C 8 F
2 1 Good luck on Monday. 2 Have a good weekend.
3 See you tomorrow. 4 Speak to you soon.

UNIT 44

1 1 c 2 c 3 b 4 a 5 b 6 b
2 1 I suggested going out for a meal.
2 She offered me a piece of cake.
3 I promised to be there by nine o'clock.
4 He apologised for being late.
5 She advised me to look for a new job.
6 I agreed to talk to her.
3 1 If I were you, I'd see a doctor.
2 I'm sorry I have to leave early.
3 Don't forget to buy the tickets.
4 Why don't we go for a swim?
5 Don't go there.
6 Would you like to come round and see the new baby?
7 I promise I'll post it for you./Don't worry, I'll post it for you, I promise.
4 1 He phoned to invite her and Ann round for dinner.
2 Next Friday./The following Friday.
5 John phoned earlier. He invited us to dinner on Saturday but I explained that our grandparents were coming to stay, so he suggested going next Friday and I accepted. He offered to come and pick us up but I reminded him that you had bought a car. Oh, he warned us not to use the A6 because of some roadworks. Anyway, I thanked him for inviting us and he apologised for not inviting/not having invited us before.

UNIT 45

1 demonstrator 2 bystander 3 police officer
2 **Police officer:** aggressive, mob, screaming, hooligans, angry
Demonstrator: wonderful, peaceful, singing, successful, jokes
3 **Example sentences:**
1 A sixty-five-year-old woman attacked two robbers when they entered her home late on Saturday night.
2 The teachers have ended their strike after one month and are returning to work on Monday.
3 A comprehensive school in West London burnt down in a huge fire early yesterday morning.
4 The Queen left London this morning for a two-week tour of Australia.

UNIT 46

1 1 was 2 had already been 3 knew 4 had never been
5 went 6 had 7 had studied 8 had 9 rained
10 were 11 had packed 12 was 13 came 14 felt
15 had had
2 Two years ago, on 1st June, it was Mrs Ambler's one hundreth birthday. She was still living at 17 Laburnum Gardens, in the house where she had lived all her life. She said she had never wanted to live anywhere else. All her memories from childhood to old age were there in that house. She had been a child there and then had had her own three children there. All of them had left many years before and her daughters were now grandmothers. Mrs Ambler's husband had died ten years before, so she had lived alone since then. She never felt lonely, however, because she had many friends and relations who came to visit her.
3 1 She is a policewoman, head of the Paris Arts Theft Squad.
2 a) Because four stolen Corot paintings had been returned to France.
b) The people who had bought the paintings in Japan.
c) Three armed criminals had hidden themselves there.
3 Five: paintings had been returned
successes had been
the people who had bought
she had finished
criminals had hidden
5 1 b 2 a 3 b 4 b 5 a

UNIT 47

1 1 Although he had a heart attack last year, he seems to be quite healthy.
In spite of having/having had a heart attack last year, he seems to be quite healthy.
2 Although she's very old now, she can still look after herself.
In spite of being very old now, she can still look after herself.
3 Although he's very intelligent, he's very boring to talk to.
In spite of being very intelligent, he's very boring to talk to.
4 Although she works very hard, she doesn't earn much money.
In spite of working very hard, she doesn't earn much money.
2 1 playwright 2 poet 3 author 4 journalist
3 2 biography 3 romantic novel 4 short stories
5 detective story 6 travel book 7 autobiography

UNIT 48

1 1 I wish we hadn't had an argument.
2 I wish I could speak English very well.
3 I wish I'd/had helped them.
4 I wish I didn't have to go to school.
5 I wish I lived near a swimming pool.
2 **Example sentences:**
I wish I had worked harder.
I wish I hadn't spent the evenings playing pinball.
I wish I had got up early in the mornings.
I wish I had gone to all the lectures.
I wish I had written an essay every week.
I wish I had revised harder for my exams.

UNIT 49

1 1 hadn't rained. . . would have gone
2 would have called round. . . had known
3 would have got. . . had applied
4 would have done. . . had known
5 hadn't seen. . . wouldn't have bought
6 would have been killed. . . hadn't been
7 wouldn't have left. . . hadn't been
2 1 if you had the money?
2 I'd/would have seen them.
3 if I'd wanted it.
4 I'll tell her the news.
5 if she knew about this letter.
6 if we don't hurry.
7 if you'd/had asked her.
3 1 It's amusing.
2 Shakespeare would have written better if he'd had a Berol.
4 1 Albert Einstein would have found the answers more quickly with a Techno Computer.
2 Florence Nightingale would have saved more lives with Allcure medicine.
3 Queen Victoria would have looked more beautiful in Goldmark designer clothes.
4 Sherlock Holmes would have been able to see better with 'Clearview' glasses.

UNIT 50

1 1 didn't you? 2 aren't you? 3 have you? 4 won't you?
5 should I? 6 had he? 7 mustn't we? 8 doesn't she?
9 were you? 10 is he?
2 **Example question:**
1 Would you rather be with him than with anyone else?
3 1 Eton 2 A musician 3 Motorcycle courier
4 The Docklands 5 Stratford-upon-Avon 6 Shakespeare
7 Jewellery maker 8 Stones 9 Ice hockey 10 They left the tickets at home.

Answer Key

UNIT 1

1 1 got 2 has been working/has worked 3 like 4 'll/will probably go 5 went 6 didn't like 7 was 8 left 9 won't send 10 'll/will send 11 didn't get 12 don't need 13 's/is studying 14 comes 15 want
2 1 D 2 C 3 E 4 G 5 F 6 A
3 1 a 2 b 3 a 4 b 5 b 6 b 7 a 8 b 9 b 10 a
4 1 approve 2 agree 3 educate 4 think 5 live
5 1 uniVERsity 2 acaDEMic 3 OPPosite 4 aNNOY 5 muSIcian 6 magaZINE 7 COMpany 8 comPUter 9 riDIculous 10 eduCAtion

UNIT 2

1 1 're/are studying 2 plays 3 visit 4 don't understand 5 Are you going out 6 's/is staying
2 1 love 2 like 3 enjoy 4 's/is 5 Do you write 6 don't know 7 's/is looking for 8 Do you play 9 'm/am learning 10 needs 11 're/are making 12 Are you rehearsing 13 're/are working 14 're/are giving 15 have to 16 Do you get on well 17 don't argue
3 1 Helen 2 Peter 3 Alice 4 Sarah
4 1 Helen is holding a ball.
She lives in Brighton.
2 Peter is running out of the water.
He plays football for his local team.
3 Alice is making a funny face.
She works in Sarah's office.
4 Sarah is reading.
She has her own business.
6 1 a 2 b 3 b 4 a 5 a

UNIT 3

1 1 compact DISC 2 ALbum 3 SINgle 4 PAPerback 5 MARker pen 6 HARDback 7 reCEIPT 8 magaZINE 9 caSSETTE 10 WRIting paper
2 1 £9.99 2 £110 3 £2 4 50p 5 £43,000

UNIT 4

1 2 You're not allowed to drink alcohol.
3 You're not allowed to smoke.
4 You're not allowed to put posters on your bedroom walls.
5 You're not allowed to have lights on after 9.30 p.m.
2 7 You're not supposed to play music in the study rooms, but everyone does.
8 You're not supposed to eat in the study rooms, but everyone does.
9 You're not supposed to talk in the library, but everyone does.
10 You're not supposed to take trips into town without permission, but everyone does.
3 1 A 2 F 3 B 4 D 5 C

UNIT 5

1 1 conformist 2 extrovert 3 tease 4 talent 5 shy
2 because and both because as well as and

UNIT 6

1 *1* came in was leaving called out started
2 saw Were they playing weren't were running Did you say shouted didn't answer didn't see
2 *1* 1 were watching 2 rang 3 went 4 opened 5 was
2 1 was sleeping 2 was 3 woke up 4 were arguing/shouting/having an argument/having a row 5 threw 6 screamed 7 was/went
3 ACROSS: 1 passport 5 take 6 lock 8 or 10 have 12 leave 14 it 15 musician 16 interview
DOWN: 2 see 3 oil 4 ticket 7 she 9 return 11 visa 13 voice
5 1 Do 2 Were 3 Is 4 Do 5 Was 6 Did 7 Are

UNIT 7

1 1 houseproud 2 homesick 3 house-warming 4 home-made
2 1 when 2 at the age of 3 at first 4 for a time 5 after 6 in 7 at 8 during 9 eventually 10 now

UNIT 8

1 1 b 2 b 3 b 4 b 5 b 6 a 7 a
2 **Example dialogue:**
ALAN: Oh no! I'm terribly sorry, Bob!
BOB: That's all right, Alan.
ALAN: Is the jacket washable?
BOB: Well no, I'm afraid it isn't.
ALAN: Oh dear! Look, I'll pay the dry cleaning bill.
BOB: No, it's O.K. Really.
ALAN: Well, I really am sorry.
BOB: Never mind. It's nothing to worry about.
4 1 a 2 b 3 b 4 a

UNIT 9

1 1 aren't used to 2 used to 3 Didn't she use to 4 am not used to 5 is used to 6 used to
2 1 used to 2 'm/am used to 3 used to 4 'm/am not used to 5 used to 6 're/are used to
3 1 F 2 T 3 T 4 F 5a F 5b T 5c T 5d T 5e F 5f T

UNIT 10

1 1 in 2 on...in 3 in 4 on 5 on 6 in
2 1 a procession of half-seen figures 2 showing the marks of our boots 3 collection of fine old china 4 But most of the time 5 potatoes of unusual shape 6 coal and sticks of beech wood 7 six tables of different sizes
3 ACROSS: 2 coal 5 piano 7 as 9 candle 10 else 14 modern 15 awake 16 pot
DOWN: 1 crackle 2 cottage 3 attic 4 sofa 5 plant 8 silent 11 low 12 to 13 nest 14 me

UNIT 11

1 1 cost of living 2 afford 3 rich 4 money 5 cost 6 pay 7 rise
2 photography acting journalism hairdressing science engineering physics

UNIT 12

1 1 's/is going to 2 will 3 'll/will 4 'll/will 5 'll/will 6 will
2 **going to:** 2 We're going to spend the whole summer by the sea.
will: 4 I'll send her a card this afternoon.
5 I'll phone every day.
6 I'll carry one for you.
7 I'll get a place at university.
8 Millions of people will die of hunger again next year.
3 1 F 2 F 3 T 4 F 5 F 6 F 7 T 8 T
5 1 b 2 a 3 a 4 b 5 a

UNIT 13

1 1 turn it down, (please)? 2 borrow yours, (please)? 3 could use yours, (please)? 4 could post it for me, (please)? 5 typing it again, (please)? 6 moving it (please)?
2 receptionist 4E receipt 2D urgent 5B deliver 1A sign 3C

UNIT 14

1 1 will be able to/can...can't 2 couldn't/wasn't able to 3 was able to 4 be able to 5 couldn't/wasn't able to 6 have been able to
2 1 could/was able to 2 could/was able to 3 was able to 4 couldn't 5 will be able to

UNIT 15

1 1 wonderful 2 delicious 3 spectacular 4 magnificent 5 fantastic
2 1 terrible 2 dreadful 3 awful
3

unhappy	incorrect	impolite	irresponsible
unable	inexpensive	imperfect	
unclear	informal	impatient	
unforgettable		improbable	

4 1 among 2 on 3 along 4 through 5 on 6 across 7 to 8 From 9 along 10 past

UNIT 16

1 1 catch 2 'll/will take 3 catch 4 'll/will arrive 5 miss...'ll/will 6 catch 7 'll/will catch
2 1 What'll you do if you can't find anywhere to stay?
2 What'll you do if you lose/spend all your money?
3 What'll you do if you're ill?
4 What'll you do if you get lost?
3 1 E 2 B 3 A 4 C 5 D
4 1 If you go by bike, you'll have to be careful.
2 If you go by underground, you'll get to your destination quickly./you won't see much of the city.
3 If you go by taxi, you'll have a very comfortable journey.
4 If you walk, you'll be able to stop and look at anything that interests you. / it'll give you a sense of the 'atmosphere' of London.
5 If you go by bus, you'll get a good view of the city.

UNIT 17

1 **Sports:** running, skiing, cycling, windsurfing, swimming, golf, skating, tennis
Places: pool, slope, ring, court, arena, pitch
2 **Example sentences:**
She plays football on Sundays.
She goes running on Mondays.
She goes cycling on Wednesdays.
She goes swimming on Thursdays.
She plays golf on Fridays.
3 Agadir 5 windsurfing, sailing, waterskiing, tennis, horseriding
Gran Canaria 6 tennis, golf, swimming, windsurfing, horseriding, camel-riding

UNIT 18

1 1 doesn't she? 2 haven't I? 3 didn't you? 4 aren't they? 5 won't you? 6 didn't you? 7 isn't he?

2 1 Doesn't she come from Italy?
2 Haven't I met you before?
3 Didn't you leave school last year?
4 Aren't they going to get married soon?
5 Won't you be twenty next birthday?
6 Didn't you use to have a car like that?
7 Isn't he supposed to be at work?

3 **Possible questions:**
1 You're a journalist, aren't you?
2 You were born in Manchester, weren't you?
3 You were born in 1960, weren't you?
4 You live in England, don't you?
5 You're 1.82 metres tall, aren't you?
6 You've got a scar on your left arm, haven't you?
7 You've got a son, haven't you?
8 His name's Colin, isn't it?
9 He was born in 1985, wasn't he?
10 You're a political correspondent, aren't you?
11 You work for The Daily News, don't you?
12 You live in Camden Town, don't you?
13 Your address is 210, Lyme St, Camden Town, isn't it?
14 Your work address is 410, Cannon St, London EC4, isn't it?

4 shallow/deep put on/take off
offer/refuse lengthy/short
sunny/cloudy simple/complicated

5 1 didn't speak was putting rang
2 Are you going to come are staying I'll try
3 were able to
4 came used to is used to
5 come 'll have
6 heard jumped ran

UNIT 19

1 1 Why don't you take some sandwiches in case there isn't a buffet car on the train?
2 Take this map in case you get lost.
3 I'll take my sunglasses in case it's sunny.
4 You should always phone before you come round in case I'm not in.
5 I always use my alarm clock in case I don't wake up.
6 I'll stay at home in case Pat calls.
7 We'll have to take out insurance in case we have an accident.

2 1C Phone me when/as soon as you arrive.
2E We'd better be quiet in case we wake the baby.
3F I'll phone you as soon as/when I get my results.
4A She should pass the exam if she works hard.
5B I'll leave this job unless they give me a rise.

UNIT 20

1 Clare Andrews, Cambridge, Hostel for the Homeless, 3rd
Tim Hunter, Brighton, Old People's Home, 4th
Alec Jones, London, Children's Hospital, 1st
John Stevens, Bristol, Animal Rescue Society, 2nd

2 **Adverbs:** badly, perfectly, noisily, lovingly, unhappily, slowly, beautifully, excitedly
Adjectives: likely, hilly, lovely, lively, jolly, friendly, lonely

UNIT 21

1 *Table 5*
1 tomato juice
1 cereal – cornflakes
1 mushrooms on toast
1 scrambled egg on toast
Toast
2 teas

2 1 getting dark. 2 getting excited. 3 getting worried. 4 getting old. 5 got accepted. 6 getting better. 7 got fired (last week). 8 get lost.

UNIT 22

1 1a ✗ b ✓ 2a ✓ b ✗ 3a ✗ b ✓ 4a ✓ b ✗ 5a ✓ b ✗ 6a ✓ b ✗
7a ✗ b ✓ 8a ✓ b ✗ 9a ✗ b ✓ 10a ✓ b ✗

2 1 What have you been doing in the last few months?
2 What other countries have you visited?
3 Have you (ever) been a waiter before?
4 What other jobs have you had?
5 Why do you want to work as a waiter?
6 How long have you been looking for a job?
7 When are you going to leave Stratford?

3 1 She hasn't written to me yet.
2 They have already done all the washing-up.
3 Have you seen that film yet?
4 Sarah has just told me the good news.
5 Haven't we already seen this programme?

4 **for:** three months, a week, ten years, a term, a few minutes, an hour and a half
since: I finished school, 1984, 3rd August, the beginning of the year, 9 o'clock, I was a child

UNIT 23

1 1 is 2 is 3 has 4 has 5 is 6 has 7 is 8 has

2 1 This soup is salty. 2 This meat is underdone. 3 This zip has broken. 4 The coffee machine doesn't work.
5 This shirt has shrunk.

3 **Example complaints and requests:**
1 I'm afraid this soup is salty. Would you mind taking it back to the kitchen?
2 I'm sorry but this meat is underdone. Would you mind grilling it for a bit longer?
3 I'm afraid this zip has broken. Could you put in a new one, please?
4 I'm afraid the coffee machine doesn't work. Could you give me my money back, please?
5 I'm afraid this shirt has shrunk. Would you mind changing it for a different one?

4 1 happy 2 naughty 3 pretty 4 silly 5 ugly

5 **Example dialogue:**
ASSISTANT: Can I help you?
ANN: Yes, I bought some trousers here last week and when I washed them, they shrank and the button came off.
ASSISTANT: Oh, I'm sorry about that.
ANN: Well, could you give me a refund, please?
ASSISTANT: I'm afraid the shop doesn't give refunds.
ANN: Well, I think you should give refunds.
ASSISTANT: Look, I'm sorry about the trousers. Shall I change them for you?
ANN: No thank you. I'd like to see the manager, please.

UNIT 24

1 **Make:** a cake, friends, a noise, a meal, a mistake, the bed, an arrangement
Do: the washing-up, my homework, my hair, some repairs, the shopping, a course, the cleaning

2 1 I've got to do the shopping.
2 I've got to make the beds.
3 I've got to do the washing-up.
4 I've got to do the cleaning.
5 I've got to make the dinner.

3 hope big work
hole bag word/fork
hold bar wood/ford
told car food

UNIT 25

1 1 f 2 c 3 g 4 i 5 e 6 d 7 h 8 b

UNIT 26

1 A news story is selected by the director and producer. Then a reporter and a camera crew are sent to the story location. The news script is written by the director and the story is told by the reporter. The film is sent to the studio by motorbike and the length of the story is agreed by the director and producer. After that, the film is cut by the director. It is then introduced by a newsreader.

2 1 A lot of T.V.s are being stolen at the moment.
2 I was never given homework when I was your age.
3 This school is going to be closed soon.
4 Do you think it will be knocked down?
5 Tea has to be made with boiling water.
6 Our rooms were being prepared when we arrived.

3 **Example article:**
At Broad Street Junior School yesterday, a dangerous snake was found in Class 6's room. It was discovered by six-year-old Renny Astley when she put her feet under her desk. After the discovery, the class were sent home for the day, the classroom was locked and the police were called. An animal rescue team was then sent from the local zoo and the snake was caught and taken to Chester Zoo. No-one knows how the snake got there. The police are now investigating. The snake was a boa constrictor and was two metres long.

UNIT 27

1 St Thomas's Hospital 7, County Hall 5, Cleopatra's Needle 2, Houses of Parliament 6, National Theatre 1, Hispaniola 3

2 1 (Texas is situated in the south-west of the USA) above Mexico and the Gulf of Mexico.
2 (It became part of the United States) in 1845.
3 (The official language is) English.
4 Spanish (is also widely spoken).
5 (A lot of) oil (is produced there).
6 (The oil is exported to) other American states.
7 (The state (is headed by a governor but) is governed by) the President of the USA and the Congress.

3 Six: is situated, is (also widely) spoken, is produced, (is) exported, is headed, is governed

5

Suzi	Hal	Mo	
Kay			Mel
			Ali
	Jo		Brad

1 Two 2 Hal 3 Ali

Unit 26

GRAMMAR: the passive

1 **Read the description below and then rewrite it using the passive. Use linking words (*and, then, after that,* etc) where necessary.**

A news story is selected by the director and producer. Then the a reporter and a camera crew are sent to the story location. The news script is written by the director and the story is told by the reporter. The film is sent to the studio by motorbike and the lenght of the story is agreed by the director and producer. After then, the film is cut by the director. It's then introduced by a newsreader.

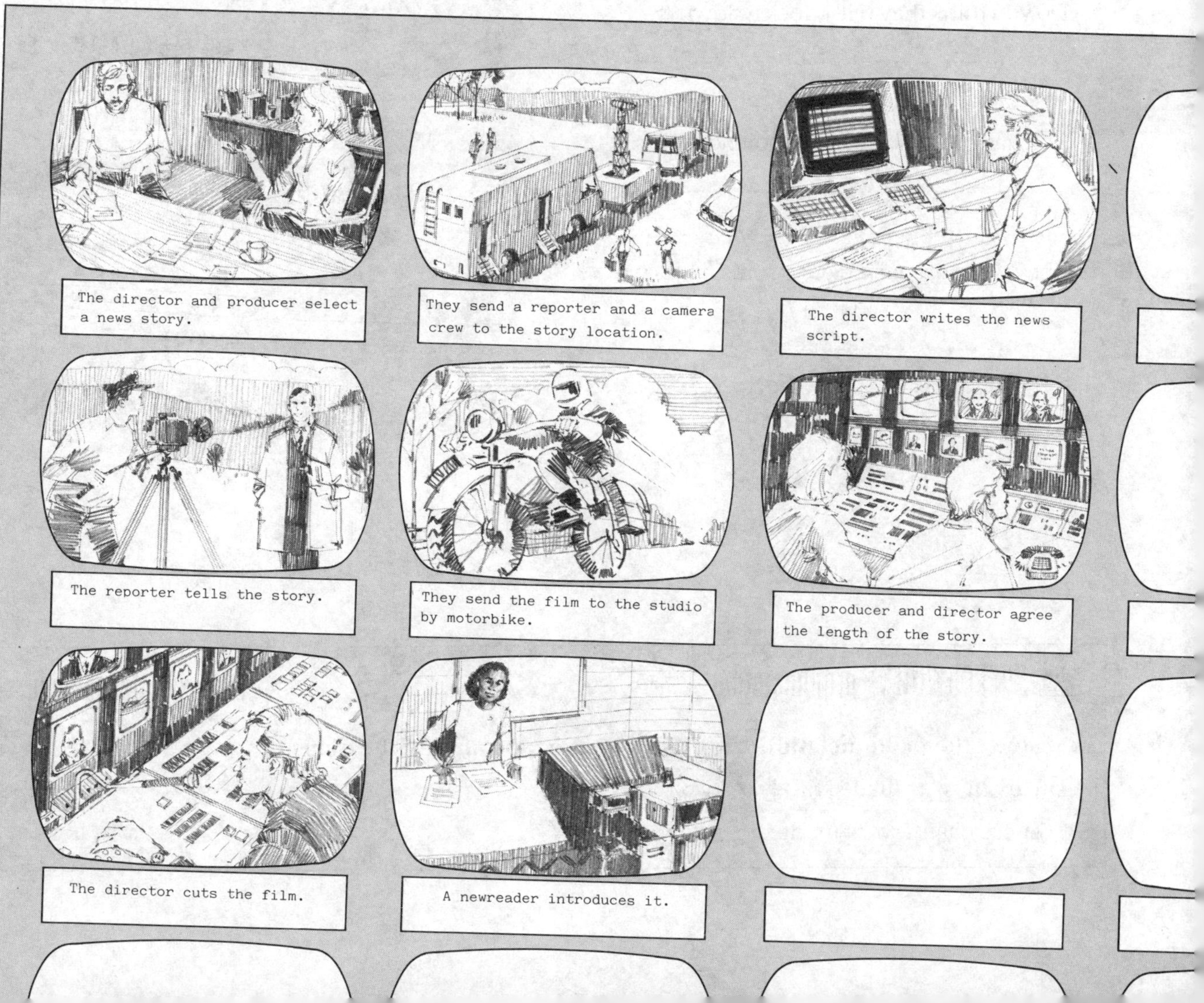

2 Rewrite the following sentences using the passive voice.

You make spaghetti from flour and water.
Spaghetti is made from flour and water.

1 People are stealing a lot of T.V.s at the moment.
A lot of TV. are being stolen at the moment

2 The teachers never gave me homework when I was your age.
I was never given homework when I was your age.

3 They're going to close this school soon.
? this school is going to be closed soon

4 Do you think they will knock it down?
Do you think it will be knocked down?

5 You have to make tea with boiling water.
Tea has to be made with boiling water.

6 They were preparing our rooms when we arrived.
Our rooms were being prepared when we arrived

WRITING

3 In your notebook, write a short newspaper article using the reporter's notes below. Give your article a headline.

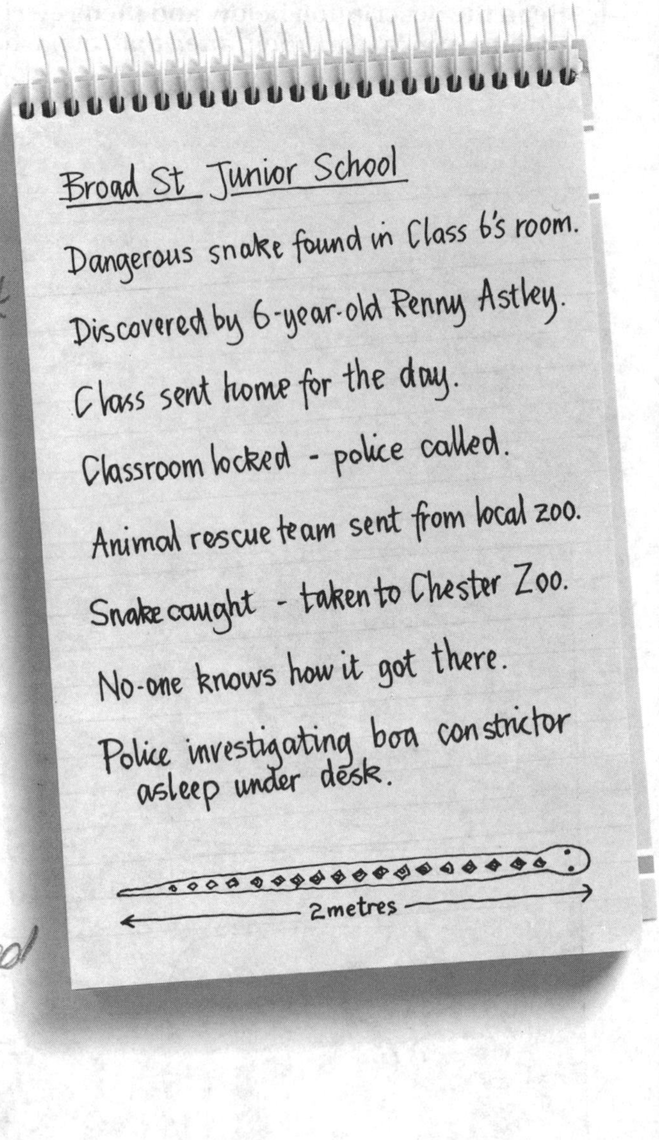

SPEECHWORK: pronunciation

Past simple passive

4 Study the pronunciation, then listen to the tape and do the drills.

This car <u>was</u> made in Italy. / wəz /

These chairs <u>were</u> made in England. / wə /

Unit 27

LISTENING

1 **Listen to the guided tour of the River Thames. Write the correct number from the map next to each location.**

Shell Building 4

St Thomas's Hospital ☐

County Hall ☐

Cleopatra's Needle ☐

Houses of Parliament ☐

National Theatre ☐

Hispaniola ☐

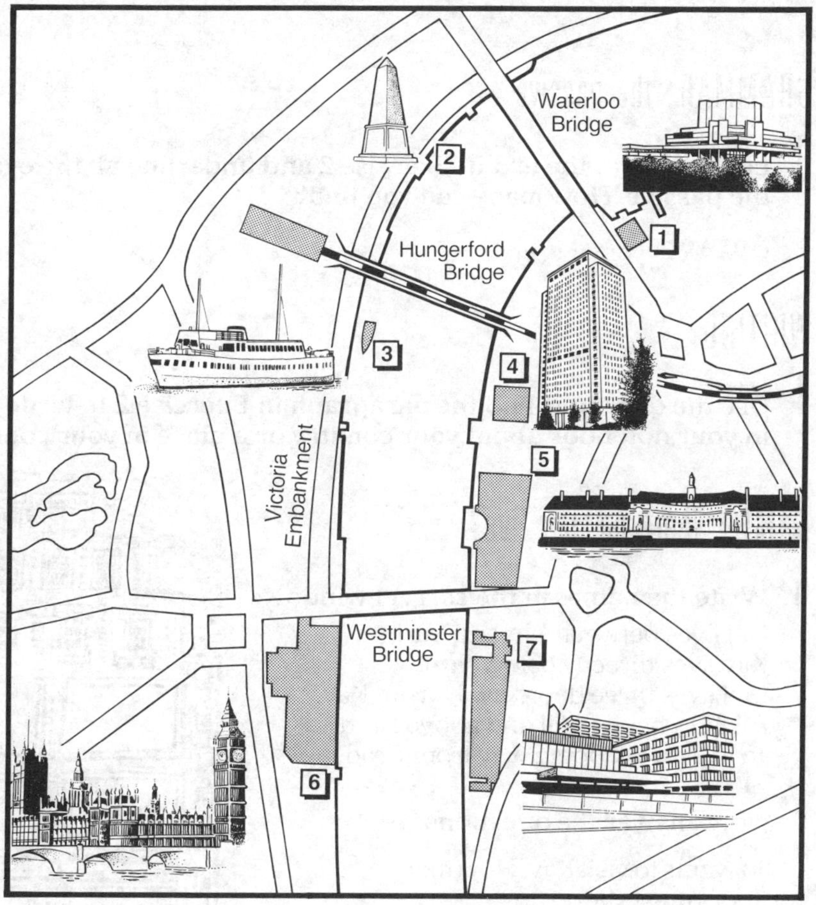

READING

2 **Read the paragraph about Texas and answer the questions.**

1 Where is it situated?

....

2 When did it become part of its present country?

....

3 What is the official language?

....

4 Are there any other languages widely spoken?

....

5 What is produced there?

....

6 Where is this product exported to?

....

7 Who is the state governed by?

....

TEXAS

THE state of Texas is a south-western state of the USA and is situated above Mexico and the Gulf of Mexico. In fact it used to be part of Mexico but became part of the United States in 1845. The official language is English, though Spanish is also widely spoken. A lot of oil is produced in Texas and exported to other American states, although this isn't the state's only business; there are many other industries too, and agriculture is also important. The state is headed by a governor, who decides local issues. As part of the USA, Texas is governed by the President and the Congress.

GRAMMAR: the passive

3 **Look again at the text in Exercise 2 and underline all the examples of the passive. How many can you find?**

Answer ....

WRITING

4 **Use the questions and the paragraph in Exercise 2 to write a paragraph in your notebook about your country or a place in your country.**

GAME: Where do they live?

5 **Write the names in the correct windows.**

Hal lives between Mo and Suzi.
Kay lives directly below Suzi.
Mel lives three doors away from Kay.
Ali lives below Mel and above Brad.
Jo lives two doors away from Brad.

Now answer the questions.

1 Jo wants to visit Kay. How many floors must she go up?

....

2 Suzi wants to borrow some sugar. Who is the nearest person to borrow it from?

....

3 There is a lot of noise coming through Brad's ceiling. Who is probably making the noise?

....

VOCABULARY: shapes

6 **In your Students' Book, the Empire State Building is described as 'rather like a pyramid'. Label the shapes below, using the words in the box.**

diamond	circle	cube	square
pyramid	rectangle	oval	triangle

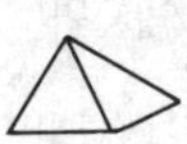
.....*pyramid*....

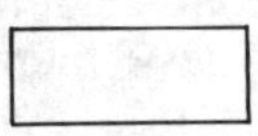
1 ....

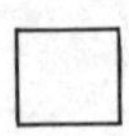
2 ....

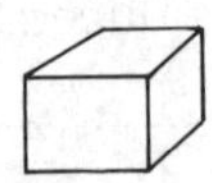
3 ....

4 ....

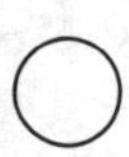
5 ....

6 ....

7 ....

Unit 28

READING

1 **Read the story about Adrian and underline the things he does which are rude in your country.**

A disastrous dinner guest

Last week Adrian Wilson was invited to dinner at his girlfriend's parents' house. He had never met them before.

He was asked to come at eight o'clock but arrived at nine. He took off his coat, went into the sitting room and sat down. He said he was thirsty and asked for a beer. When he had finished his beer, everyone got up to go to the dinner table. Adrian was served first. While the others were waiting for their soup, Adrian started his. When he had finished, he asked for some more. After his soup, he lit up a cigarette and poured himself another glass of wine. During the main course, he said he'd just remembered something and he got up to make a phone call. When he got back, he said he had to leave straight away and said goodbye to everyone.

COMMUNICATION: obligation and prohibition

2 **Look at Exercise 1 and write five sentences of advice to Adrian about social behaviour, using *You're expected to, You're not supposed to,* or *You shouldn't.***

You're expected to arrive on time for dinner.

1 ……………………………………………

2 ……………………………………………

3 ……………………………………………

4 ……………………………………………

5 ……………………………………………

SPEECHWORK: stress and intonation

Obligation and prohibition

3 **Study the stress and intonation, then listen to the tape and do the drills.**

Do we HAVE to stay to the END?

You're exPECted to make a SPEECH.

You're NOT supposed to SMOKE on the UNderground.

itness
s to do it.

entre
be.)

Unit 29

GRAMMAR: relative pronouns

1 Complete the paragraph, using *who, which, where, whose,* or leaving a blank.

BILLIE HOLIDAY

American singer (1913 – 1959)

Billie Holiday is a show-business figure ..*who*.. will never be forgotten. She was one of the greatest nightclub singers [1] ....the world has ever known. She heard her first jazz music in the Baltimore club [2] ....she used to sing as a child. She became a successful jazz singer and later toured with a man [3] ....band was well-known all over the world – Count Basie.

Holiday had the sort of voice [4] .... made songs like 'The man I love' unforgettable. However, her personal life was never happy. The man [5] ....she really loved was her first husband, a heroin addict. It was her attempt to cure him [6] .... caused her own addiction and [7] ....turned her life into a pattern of hospital and prison.

2 In each sentence below, the relative clause is in *italics.* Is the relative pronoun in the box the subject or the object of each clause? Write S or O.

She's the woman [that] *I met this morning.* — O

I'd like to live in a town [which] *had a good night life.* — S

1 That's the woman [who] *'s left her husband.* — ☐

2 This is the shop [that] *I described to you.* — ☐

3 This is the friend [who] *I knew as a child.* — ☐

4 Let me introduce you to the man [who] *taught me Russian.* — ☐

5 This is the house [that] *we're going to buy.* — ☐

6 I'd prefer to see a film [which] *has a happy ending.* — ☐

3 Rewrite the sentences in Exercise 2 which contain object relative pronouns, omitting the pronoun.

She's the woman I met this morning.

....

....

....

Unit 30

CROSSWORD

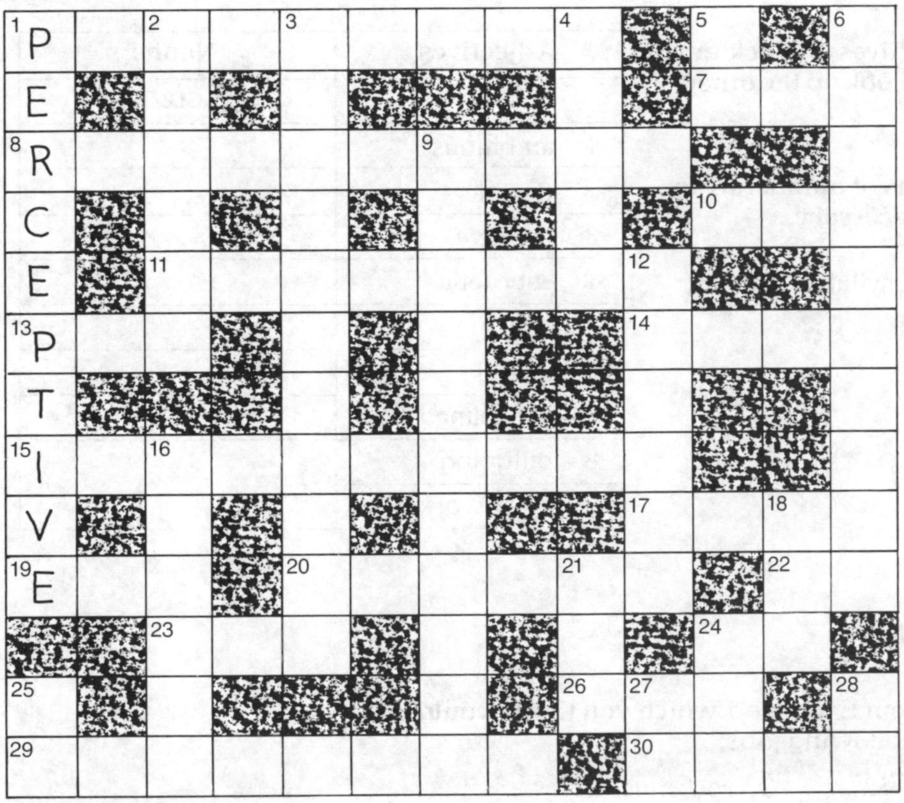

ACROSS

1 *How to be an alien* was ... in 1946. (9)
7 *Also* (3)
8 I like cold drinks – they're very .... (10)
10 He's the man ... sold me the tickets. (3)
11 She's a .... She works for the *New York Times*. (8)
13 I had apple ... and cream for pudding. (3)
14 Have you ... been to New York? (4)
15 Texas has many ..., but the biggest is oil. (10)
17 Would you give it to us, please – it's ... (4)
19 I can't hear very well – there's something wrong with my left .... (3)
20 He can play the piano and the .... (6)
22 They came ... quickly as they could. (2)
23 Would you like some ... in your drink? (3)
24 I left the keys ... the table. (2)
26 The bridge was too .... The bus couldn't go under it. (3)
29 In Britain, people can vote when they're .... (8)
30 He was frightened. I could hear the ... in his voice. (4)

DOWN

1 Showing an unusual ability to notice and understand. (10)
2 Opposite of *after*. (6)
3 Cheap. (11)
4 Would you like to ... ? No thanks, I don't like this music very much. (5)
5 I'm staying ... the Majestic Hotel. (2)
6 Having no colour. (10)
9 We went to the cinema to see a .... (6, 5)
12 I had a good ... for being late. (6)
16 We met ... the holidays. (6)
18 Past tense of *run*. (3)
21 I had eaten too much and I felt .... (3)
24 They ... the bank a lot of money. (3)
25 It's mine. Can you give it to ..., please. (2)
27 ... course it's my money! (2)
28 Shall we stay at home, ... go out? (2)

Unit 31

VOCABULARY: personal qualities

1 **Look at the list of adjectives and tick the ones which you know. Look up the others in a dictionary.**

Write in the noun forms of numbers 1 to 7. Use a dictionary if necessary.

Underline the stressed syllable in each adjective and noun.

	Adjectives	Nouns
	efficient	*efficiency*
1	ambitious	
2	flexible	
3	creative	
4	energetic	
5	patient	
6	tactful	
7	disciplined	
8	outgoing	
9	hard-working	

WRITING: personal qualities

2 **Write one adjective from Exercise 1 which you think would be useful for each of the following jobs.**

teacher *patient*
1 police officer ....
2 secretary ....
3 rock musician ....
4 writer ....
5 nurse ....
6 actor ....
7 diplomat ....
8 politician ....

3 **Using an adjective and a noun from Exercise 1, write a sentence for four of the jobs as in the example.**

A teacher has to be patient, and flexibility is also important.

1 ....
2 ....
3 ....
4 ....

LISTENING

4 **Choose which jobs the women on the tape are talking about and write them below.**

nurse politician secretary writer

1 *secretary* 2 .... 3 .... 4 ....

Unit 32

GRAMMAR: first and second conditional

1 Complete the sentences by writing the verbs in the correct form, using the second conditional.

If I (live) *lived* nearer to my parents, I (go) *would go* to see them more often.

1 If I (have) .... a degree, I (apply) .... for that job.

2 What (you / do) .... if you (see) .... someone stealing from a shop?

3 I (help) .... her if I (have) .... the time.

4 If I (be) .... you, I (change) .... jobs.

5 If you (have) .... a lot of money, where (you / live) .... ?

6 I (go) .... swimming if there (be) .... a pool nearby.

7 It (be) .... a nice place for a holiday if you (have) .... children.

8 I (go out) .... tonight if I (not / be) .... so tired.

9 She (do) .... well if she (work) .... harder.

10 She (not marry) .... him if she (not love) .... him.

2 Write sentences in the first or second conditional, as appropriate.

(sunny tomorrow)

If it's sunny tomorrow, I'll go to the beach.

1 (be the Prime Minister)

....

2 (pass my exams)

....

3 (have time this weekend)

....

4 (own a yacht)

....

5 (speak English fluently)

....

6 (rain next Saturday)

....

Enormous Walter has more than a slim chance of success

Many of us feel we have to lose a bit of weight from time to time, but Walter Hudson thinks it will take him three years to lose his extra kilos – because he's 380 kilograms overweight.

Enormous Walter, who weighs an astonishing 443 kg, is believed to be the world's heaviest man. Now, however, the 1.8-metre-tall, 42-year-old New Yorker has decided to go on a diet.

Out will go the thirty-two sausages, half a kilo of bacon, twelve eggs, loaf of bread and pot of jam that he's used to having for breakfast; the eight portions of burgers and chips that he has for lunch and the five steaks and whole apple pie that make up an average dinner.

In will come a 1,900-calorie-a-day mix of fruit and nuts. And he'll have to have more exercise – he's so huge that he's left his home only once in twenty-seven years and spends his time lying in bed. He'll probably need some new interests to take his mind off food and get him out of bed. And we suggest he gives himself a target of how much he wants to lose each week. Three years is a long time to be on such a strict diet. Well, Walter, the best of luck!

READING

3 Read the article and answer the questions.

1 How much does Walter weigh? ....

2 How much should he weigh, according to the text? ....

3 How long does he think it will take to lose his extra weight? ....

4 Until now, what has he usually had for breakfast? ....

....

5 What kind of food is he going to eat now? ....

6 What does he spend most of his time doing? ....

4 In your notebook, write four sentences of advice for Walter, starting with *If I were you*.

If I were you, I'd get out of bed more often.

SPEECHWORK: pronunciation

Would and will contractions

5 Study the pronunciation, then listen to the tape and do the drills.

If she loses her job, she'll move out of London. / ʃil /
If she lost her job, she'd move out of London. / ʃid /

6 Listen and write the correct word: *will* or *would*.

would	2	4
1	3	5

Unit 33

COMMUNICATION: polite requests for information

1 Write polite requests for information, using *Could you tell me* or *Do you know*.

Q: *Could you tell me when the next class starts?*

A: On 1st June.

1 Q: ....

A: Oh yes, we have three certificate classes.

2 Q: ....

A: Oh, about forty.

3 Q: ....

A: A maximum of eighteen.

4 Q: ....

A: Oh yes, of course.

5 Q: ....

A: At nine o'clock.

SPEECHWORK: stress and intonation

Requests for information

2 Study the stress and intonation, then listen to the tape and do the drills.

COULD you tell me what his WORK number is, PLEASE?

Have you any iDEa when he'll be BACK?

Do you KNOW if he received a PARcel this MORning?

3 Listen to the requests and write the one which sounds more polite, a or b.

☑ *b* 1 ☐ 2 ☐ 3 ☐ 4 ☐

Unit 34

VOCABULARY

1 **Match the nouns from the box with the verbs on the right. (Sometimes more than one noun is possible.)**

car	television
hair	telephone
dress	flat
tyres	jacket

dry clean – *dress, jacket*
check – car,
install – tyres,
cut – hair
repair – television, telephone
service – car, television
decorate – flat
alter – jacket

GRAMMAR: *have/get something done*

2 **Write a sentence for each verb in Exercise 1 using *get something done*, or *have something done*. Start with *I'm going to....***

I'm going to get my dress dry cleaned.

1 I'm going to get my car check.
2 I'm going to get my tyres install.
3 I'm going to get my cut hair.
4 I'm going to get a telephone repair.
5 I'm going to get a television service.
6 I'm going to get my flat decorate.
7 I'm going to get my jacket alter.

GAME

3 **Circle the odd word out in each box.**

suit blouse socks hair

1 kitchen garden bedroom living-room

2 attractive good-looking plain pretty

3 clouds snow rain hail

4 potato onion apple cauliflower

5 butter eggs cream cheese

Unit 35

VOCABULARY: adjectives

Some adjectives have very strong meanings, and cannot be preceded by *very*. (You can say: *She's wonderful*, but not *She's very wonderful*.)

1 Circle the words that cannot be preceded by *very*:

outstanding	bad	brilliant	impossible	terrific	competitive
beautiful	tired	fantastic	ruthless	essential	terrible
disgusting	strong	tough	awful	important	nice

LISTENING

2 Before listening, look at the domestic jobs below. Which do you think are done by women and which by men? Then listen and match the jobs with the people.

Ellen's mother

- cooking
- cleaning
- washing-up
- shopping
- repairs
- gardening
- car washing
- car maintenance
- decorating
- packing
- looking after children

Ellen's father

REVISION: second conditional questions

3 Write questions for these answers using the second conditional.

What would you do if you won £1,000?

I'd spend it on a holiday.

1 ....

Maybe I'd go and live with my mother. But I don't think my parents will ever get divorced.

2 ....

Oh, they'd be really angry. Eleven o'clock or midnight is O.K., but not three o'clock in the morning.

3 ....

I'd let them take my money and then I'd phone the police.

4 ....

I'd get out of the house straight away, trying not to breathe in any smoke.

Unit 36

GRAMMAR: *should (not) have/ought (not) to have* (simple and continuous)

1 Write sentences using *should (not) have* or *ought (not) to have*.

He didn't get there on time, so he missed the beginning.
He should have got there on time.

You weren't listening to what I said. That's why you don't understand.
You should have been listening to what I said.

1 They drank all the milk, so there isn't any for the coffee.
They shouldn't have been drinking all the milk.

2 She didn't work very hard, but I think she regrets it now.
She should have been working hardly.

3 We spent all the money yesterday, so we can't go out today.
We shouldn't have been spent all money yesterday.

4 Of course they were punished. They were smoking in the classroom.
They shouldn't have been smoking in the classroom.

5 He was lying in bed at 11.00 and his interview was at 11.30.
He should have been lying in bed at 11.00

6 I wasn't working when the boss came into the office.
I should have been working when the boss came into the office

GAME

2 Make a word from each group of letters.

d h e e a c a h	*headache*	y e d t e a i m l i m	3 immediaty
s e s s l g a	1 glasses	e t e o r s	4 stereo
d t e n a t n a t	2 atendent	l o f o h i s	5 foolish
		r l a t s e p	6 plaster

GRAMMAR: *should (not) have*

3 **Read Sarah's account of her job interview and write six sentences about what she did wrong. Use *should (not) have* + past participle, or *should (not) have been* + *ing*.**

She should have used an alarm clock.

1 She shouldn't have worn jeans

2 She should have taken a bus

3 She shouldn't have been eating crisps when the manager came in

4 She should have thought about what to say before the interview

5 She should have listened more carefully to the manager's questions

6 She shouldn't have asked only about the pay and the holidays

I had an interview for a job as a clerk in a local bank last week. The interview was at nine o'clock in the morning, which is a bit early for me, and I didn't wake up till nearly nine. I just put on my jeans, as usual. I got on my bike and started cycling but a few yards down the road I got a puncture. I couldn't mend it, so I wheeled it back to my house and then got the bus into town. By the time I arrived at the bank, it was nearly ten o'clock. I was asked to wait in the manager's office. I felt really hungry, so I started eating some crisps I'd bought on the way. I was still eating these when the manager came in, so I offered her one but she refused.

She started asking me questions about why I wanted to work in a bank but I hadn't really thought about it, so I didn't know what to say. And I wasn't really listening very carefully because I felt tired, so I didn't understand her questions. I asked her how much the pay was and how long the holidays were. She told me but she seemed a bit irritated.

At the end of the interview she asked me if I had any questions. I said: 'Yes, have I got the job?' but she said they'd let me know the following week. Well, I've just got the letter and they turned me down!

SPEECHWORK: pronunciation

Should have/ought to have

4 **Study the pronunciation, then listen to the tape and do the drills.**

We should have left earlier. / ʃʊdəv /
He ought to have phoned before. / ɔːtʊəv /
You shouldn't have talked for so long. / ʃʊdntəv /

5 **Listen to the sentences and tick the one which you hear.**

a) I should have eaten that meal. [ ]
b) I shouldn't have eaten that meal. [✓]

1 a) She should have gone to the party. [ ]
b) She shouldn't have gone to the party. [✓]

2 a) You should have run faster. [✓]
b) You should run faster. [ ]

3 a) You ought to have come earlier. [ ]
b) You ought to come earlier. [✓]

4 a) We shouldn't have told them our plans. [ ]
b) We should have told them our plans. [✓]

5 a) You shouldn't have hit that child. [✓]
b) You shouldn't hit that child. [ ]

Unit 37

REVISION: verb tenses

1 Complete the sentences with the correct tense and form of the verbs, choosing from the following tenses: present simple, present continuous, present perfect simple, past simple, *going to* future, *will* future.

A: Hello, nice to see you again. I (not see) ...*haven't seen*....... you for ages.

B: No, I (not live) 1.............................. here anymore. I (get) 2........... a job in Scotland a few months ago.

A: Oh, how nice. So what (you / do) 3 .... here now?

B: I (visit) 4.......................... my parents for a few days, but I (go) 5.......................... back to Scotland next week.

A: So what (be) 6........... your new job?

B: I've got a job as an electrician in Edinburgh.

A: Edinburgh – ooh, lovely!

B: (You / ever / be) 7.. there?

A: No, I (not) 8.................., but I (often hear) 9... how beautiful it is. My mother (live) 10................ there when she (be) 11........... a child. So what are your plans now? How long (you stay) 12.. in Edinburgh?

B: I (not know) 13.............................. but I (think) 14................ I (be) 15 .... there for quite a long time.

A: Well, maybe I (come) 16.......................... and visit you there one day.

VOCABULARY

2 Match each verb with a noun.

	Verbs			**Nouns**
	make	*B*	A	truth
1	solve	☐	B	recommendation
2	pay	☐	C	mess
3	tell	☐	D	problem
4	get into	☐	E	bill

COMPOUND WORDS

3 **In Unit 37 of your Students' Book, Cathy makes a *half-hearted* recommendation. There are other compound words with *half*. Match the words and definitions on the right.**

half-hearted → D
1 half-sister
2 half-baked
3 half board
4 half term
5 half time
6 halfway

A *n* [U] *esp. BrE* (in lodgings, hotels, etc.) the providing of a bed and either the midday meal or the evening meal as well as breakfast

B *n* [U] (in Britain) a short holiday, usu. two or three days, in the middle of a school TERM

C *adj, adv* **1** at the midpoint between two things: *The runners reached the* [redacted] *mark in the race after 49 seconds.* [+*adv/prep*] *Oxford is* [redacted] *between London and Stratford-on-Avon.* | *I was* [redacted] *to the office when I realized I'd forgotten my briefcase.* | *She'd got* [redacted] *through the book by lunch-time.*

D *adj* (of a person or action) showing little effort and no real interest: *The children made a* [redacted] *attempt to tidy their room.* — ~**ly** *adv* — ~**ness** *n* [U]

E *n* a sister related through one parent only

F *adj infml* (esp. of an idea, suggestion, etc.) stupid; not properly planned or thought about: *Another of her* [redacted] *schemes!*

G *n* [U] the short period of rest between two parts of a game, such as a football match: *The referee blew his whistle for* [redacted]. | *They were leading by two goals at* [redacted].

WRITING: sentence connectors

4 **Connect the sentences in the two columns, using *however, so,* or *because*. You may need to write them as one sentence or two.**

I'm trying to learn some Hungarian.	I really like her now.
1 I'm feeling really tired today.	I've spent all my money.
2 They've got very little money.	I'm going to Hungary for my holidays next year.
3 I didn't like Sue when I first met her.	They seem very happy.
4 I can't do any shopping today.	He'll have to take them again.
5 Jerry's failed his exams.	I must go to bed early tonight.

I'm trying to learn some Hungarian, because I'm going to Hungary for my holidays next year.

1 ....

2 ....

3 ....

4 ....

5 ....

Unit 38

READING

1 Read the text and answer the questions.

1 Where does Sharon work?

....

2 What's her job there?

....

3 How does she usually stop fights?

....

4 Does she have to use force very much?

....

5 What method of self-defence does she use?

....

Glossary:
Bouncer: someone who is employed at a club or restaurant to remove people and to stop any fights.
Minder: someone who is employed to protect another person.

WOMAN OF THE WEEK

SHARON SEXTON

She's thrown Sean Penn over her shoulder and she's asked Andrew Ridgeley to be quiet. She's slim, attractive and 1.75 metres tall. Sharon Sexton is not what most of us imagine a bouncer to look like but that's just what she is at the London club, Xenon.

'I work in the bar and dance-floor areas,' says Sharon, aged twenty-nine. 'The aim is not to be noticed. I have to move around and mix in with the crowds. I'm there to make sure no trouble starts. If anyone looks angry I just go and ask them to keep calm. Most men are so surprised at being spoken to by a woman bouncer that they don't argue. I only very occasionally have to use force.'

Sharon has also worked as a 'minder' for Madonna and for Al Pacino. She spends a lot of time practising Wing Chun, a method of self-defence designed for women.

COMMUNICATION: asking for advice and clarification

2 When a new woman bouncer started at the club, she asked Sharon for advice. Rewrite her questions, using *I don't know what to* or *I don't know whether to*.

What should I wear? *I don't know what to wear.*

1 Should I look aggressive or not? ....

2 What should I say to someone arguing? ....

3 Should I talk to people or not? ....

4 What should I do if there's a fight? ....

5 Should I use force or not? ....

SPEECHWORK: stress and intonation — Asking for advice and help

3 Study the stress and intonation, then listen to the tape and do the drills.

I don't know whether to TYPE it or NOT.

Unit 39

GRAMMAR: *could/might/must/can't have* (simple and continuous)

1 Rewrite the following sentences using *might/could/must/can't have.*

I'm sure she already knew about it.

She must have already known about it.

Perhaps she was having a bath.

She might have been having a bath.

1 It's impossible that she saw you.

....

2 Perhaps she left it at home.

....

3 You've met Helen before, of course.

....

4 It's obvious that they were watching us.

....

5 Perhaps they were sitting in the garden.

....

6 I'm sure she hasn't been working all night.

....

WRITING

2 Why does he look so depressed, do you think? Write your ideas. Where appropriate, use *might / must / could / can't.*

....

....

....

....

....

SPEECHWORK: pronunciation

Could/might/must/can't have

3 Study the pronunciation, then listen to the tape and do the drills.

could have	/ kʊdəv /	must have	/ mʌstəv /
might have	/ maɪtəv /	can't have	/ kɑːntəv /

READING

4 **Read the text and answer the questions.**

WHAT HAPPENED TO THE DINOSAURS?

A number of different theories have been proposed to explain the death of the dinosaur. We know that about thirty species lived in North America from 120 to 200 million years ago. We also know that the dinosaur was not a very intelligent animal – most dinosaurs had very small brains – and that they lived on earth for 100 million years. What we don't know is why they suddenly disappeared. Obviously something very unusual happened to cause their death.

There are a lot of possibilities. One is that North America was hit by an enormous drought. However, bones from thirty-five dinosaur species have just been discovered in China, and they died at the same time as the American animals, so it seems very unlikely that drought was responsible. It was a world problem, not a local one, that killed them all.

The popular idea that human beings killed the dinosaur is also wrong. Humans didn't arrive until a million years ago. Acid rain, surprisingly, is one of the newer theories. It is possible that pollution from acid rain was caused by a meteor crashing into the earth.

Changes in climate might also have been responsible. Either an ice age (there have been two ice ages since then) or an increase in world temperatures could have been enough to kill the dinosaurs. Anyway, there is a lesson here for human beings. If the dinosaurs can all disappear, so can we.

Are these statements true or false? Write T or F.

1 Most people agree about why the dinosaurs disappeared. ☐
2 Dinosaurs lived more than 100 million years ago. ☐
3 A number of different types of dinosaur lived in China. ☐
4 Dinosaurs were highly intelligent. ☐
5 Human beings killed the dinosaur. ☐
6 Drought probably wasn't responsible for their death. ☐
7 A sudden warming of the world might have killed them. ☐
8 A meteor definitely was not responsible for their death. ☐

GRAMMAR: *could/might/must/can't have*

5 **Using the text in Exercise 4, complete the sentences with *could / might / must / can't have*.**

The dinosaurs ....*can't have*.... died as a result of an American drought because Chinese dinosaurs died at the same time.

1 Dinosaur bones have been discovered in China, so dinosaurs .... lived there.
2 The dinosaurs all died at the same time, so something very unusual .... happened to cause their death. It .... happened by chance.
3 Human beings .... killed the dinosaur because they didn't exist until millions of years after the dinosaur had died.
4 Dinosaurs .... died because of acid rain.
5 An increase in temperature .... killed them.

Unit 40

VOCABULARY: food

1 **Choose adjectives from the list to describe the foods in the table. An adjective may be used more than once.**

mild tender ripe fatty oily sour spicy sweet
hard lean juicy tough salty strong hot

ripe, sour, sweet, hard, juicy	apple		meat
	orange		fish
	cheese		curry

PREPOSITIONS OF TIME: *at/in/on*

2 **Which prepositions precede the following words and phrases? Write them in the correct box.**

the winter 30th September 7.30 Friday August bedtime 9 o'clock 1988
the morning my first day at school New Year's Day the 1930s your birthday
the beginning of the lesson the twentieth century

At	In	On
7.30	*the winter*	*30th September*

REVISION

3 **Complete the text with one word for each gap.**

Angeliki is a student *from* Greece. She went [1] .... England four months [2] .... to study English. She is going [3] .... stay there [4] .... another six months. [5] .... she arrived, she took a room in a hotel but she hardly [6] .... practised her English there [7] .... she found a room [8] .... a house belonging [9] .... an English family. She's now hoping [10] .... stay with the family [11] .... she leaves England. She goes to a language school in the centre [12] .... town and travels there [13] .... tube. It [14] .... her about three-quarters [15] .... an hour [16] .... that's normal in London and she's [17] .... to the travelling now. Her English is [18] .... better now but she still [19] .... a lot [20] .... mistakes!

Unit 41

VOCABULARY: idiomatic language

1 Match the idiomatic expressions on the left with the correct meaning on the right.

	to catch up on → B	A	to become in the end
1	to end up	B	to do something now that you should have done earlier
2	off duty	C	to watch carefully
3	to chat	D	to be suddenly asked to go to work (e.g. doctors, police officers)
4	to keep your eyes open	E	to find out for certain
5	to be called out	F	to talk informally
6	to make sure	G	not at work (e.g. nurses, doctors, police officers)

WRITING

2 Read the extract from a letter. Think of another job and make notes about its advantages and disadvantages, then write two paragraphs about it, using linking devices like those below.

firstly secondly

lastly however

another thing is

Being a police officer is a good job. Firstly, the work is useful and you feel you're doing something for society. Secondly, you have the chance to meet a lot of different types of people. Also, there is variety in the work and you don't have to do the same thing every day. Lastly, the pay is good and you have a lot of opportunities for promotion.

However, the irregular hours can be quite a disadvantage. It's very difficult to have a social life or to see your family when you're on night shift. And another thing is that police work can be dangerous at times.

Unit 42

GRAMMAR: reported speech

1 Report what the people said.

'It's a beautiful place to visit.'

She said *that it was a beautiful place to visit.* ....

1 'We spent a week there.'

She told me ....

2 'We're going to the same place next year.'

She told me ....

3 'Have you ever thought of going there?'

She asked me ....

4 'We may go there one day.'

I told her ....

5 'You can join us next year.'

She said ....

Reported questions

2 Helen returns home very late from an evening out and her parents have a lot of questions to ask.

Where have you been?

1 Why are you so late?

2 How did you get home?

3 What have you been doing?

4 Did you go out with Jo again?

5 When are you going to do your homework?

6 Are you staying in tomorrow night?

The next day, Helen tells Jo what her parents asked. Report the questions.

They asked me where I had been. ....

1 ....

2 ....

3 ....

4 ....

5 ....

6 ....

READING

3 **Read the brochure extract and answer the questions.**

> # Sunnyside Summer Camp
>
> ### Do you want to have a good holiday and improve your English at the same time?
>
> Then come to our summer camp. You will stay in beautiful chalets only 100 metres from a long sandy beach – perfect for swimming! There are three hours of English lessons every morning, given by qualified, experienced teachers, all of whom are native speakers of English. A wide range of activities is arranged for the afternoons and evenings – games, sports competitions, excursions, discos, etc. If you prefer, you can find your own entertainment in the nearby town. It's lively, full of things to do and only ten minutes' walk from the camp.
>
> **For more information, write to:**
> **Sunnyside Summer Camp Worthing East Sussex**

1 What is the advertisement for?

....

2 What do you do in the mornings at the camp?

....

3 Where can you swim?

....

4 How far away is the town?

....

GRAMMAR: reported statements

4 **You stayed at Sunnyside Camp, featured in Exercise 3, and everything was different to the brochure's description. Using your imagination, complain in your notebook about five things mentioned in the brochure and say what actually happened.**

The brochure said that we would sleep in beautiful chalets but we had to sleep in tents.

Unit 43

COMMUNICATION: closing strategies

1 Put the conversation between Judy and Annabel in the correct order.

1	2	3	4	5	6	7	8
G							

A Listen, why don't we meet for lunch next week and you can tell me all about this man?

B Yes, it was, and I met a wonderful man there. Judy, I think I'm in love. His name's Alan.

C Yes, Wednesday will be fine. I'll see you then.

D A holiday romance? How nice! I'd love to hear about it Annabel but actually I've got some shopping to do now.

E Yes, that would be nice. What about Wednesday? At about 1 o'clock?

F O.K. Bye for now and have a good evening.

G It sounds a great holiday.

H Yes, and I suppose I ought to get back to work.

2 Choose the correct phrase from the box for the situations below.

Have a good weekend.
Take care.
Good luck on Monday.
See you tomorrow.
Speak to you soon.

Your friend is going off on holiday on her own.

Take care ....

1 Your friend has got exams on Monday.

....

2 It's Friday afternoon.

....

3 Today's Saturday. You're going to see your friend on Sunday.

....

4 You intend to phone your friend again soon.

....

SPEECHWORK: stress and intonation

Closing strategies

3 Study the stress and intonation, then listen to the tape and do the drills.

WELL, I suPPOSE I ought to get ON. LISTen, WHY don't we meet for LUNCH?

Unit 44

GRAMMAR: verbs of reporting

1 Finish each sentence correctly, choosing a, b or c.

She asked *them to stop the noise.* ....
a) them to stop the noise b) them stopping the noise c) that they stopped the noise

1 She suggested ....
a) to talk to the director b) me to talk to the director c) talking to the director

2 I invited ....
a) them for staying b) that they should stay c) them to stay

3 You said ....
a) me to come b) that I could come c) me that I could come

4 We persuaded ....
a) him to come b) that he would come c) him coming

5 They agreed ....
a) helping b) to help c) me to help

6 You should apologise ....
a) forgetting the appointment b) for forgetting the appointment
c) her to forget the appointment

2 Write the sentences in reported speech, using the correct form of each verb in the box once only.

advise	persuade	offer	agree
suggest	promise	apologise	

ALICE: Oh, go on, please stay with me.

JANE: All right, I'll stay.

Alice *persuaded Jane to stay with her.* ....

1 'Why don't we go out for a meal?'

I ....

2 'Would you like a piece of cake?'

She ....

3 'Don't worry, I'll be there by nine o'clock, I promise.'

I ....

4 'I'm sorry I'm late.'

He ....

5 'If I were you, I'd look for a new job.'

She ....

6 'O.K., I'll talk to her.'

I ....

3 Write these sentences as direct speech.

She offered me a cup of tea. *Would you like a cup of tea?*

1 I advised her to see a doctor.

2 He apologised for having to leave early.

3 I reminded her to buy the tickets.

4 He suggested going for a swim.

5 They warned us not to go there.

6 They invited us to go round and see the new baby.

7 She promised to post that letter for me.

WRITING: summarising conversations

4 Read the telephone conversation and answer the questions.

JOHN: Hello, Helen? Is that you?
HELEN: Yes.
JOHN It's John here. I was wondering if you and Ann would like to come round for dinner on Saturday.
HELEN: That's very nice of you John, but our grandparents are coming to stay this weekend.
JOHN: Oh, O.K. Well, how about next week, say ... Friday?
HELEN: Yes, we'd love to come next Friday.
JOHN: Great. Shall I come and pick you up?
HELEN: No, there's no need. Don't you remember? Ann bought a car a couple of months ago.
JOHN: Oh, yes, so she did. Oh, make sure you don't use the A6. There are roadworks there at the moment.
HELEN: O.K. Well, thanks for inviting us, John.
JOHN: Not at all. I'm sorry I haven't invited you before. I know I said I was going to invite you ages ago.

1 Why has John phoned Helen? ....

2 When do they make the arrangement for? ....

5 Helen later summarises the conversation to her sister Ann. In your notebook, write what she says, using the verbs below.

explain thank suggest accept invite warn remind offer apologise

Start like this:

John phoned earlier. He invited us to dinner on Saturday but I explained that our grandparents were coming to stay, so he

Unit 45

LISTENING

1 **Listen to three people describing a demonstration: a police officer, a demonstrator and a bystander (= someone who was watching but not involved). Match the people with their descriptions on the tape.**

Description: 1 .... 2 .... 3 ....

2 **The words below were used by either the police officer or the demonstrator. Write them in the correct box.**

threatening positive wonderful aggressive peaceful mob
screaming singing hooligans successful angry jokes

Police officer	Demonstrator
threatening	*positive*

WRITING

3 **Write the first sentence of the article for each of the following headlines.**

Prince Charles opened a new hospital in London yesterday.

1 ....
....

3 ....
....

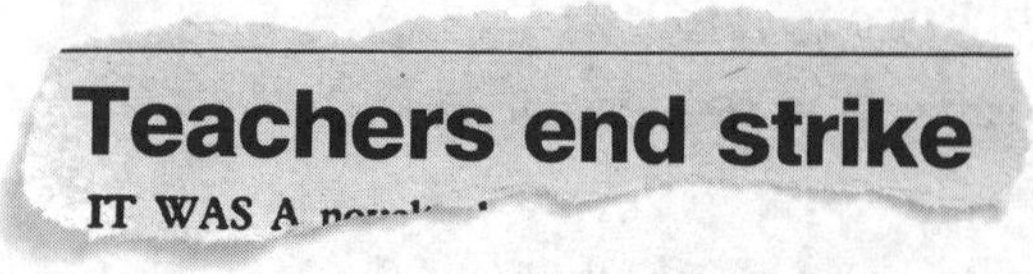

2 ....
....

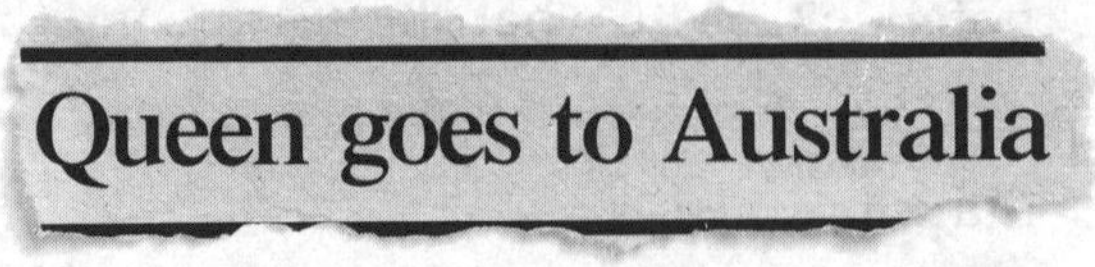

4 ....
....

Unit 46

GRAMMAR: past perfect and past simple

1 Complete the text using the correct form of the past perfect or past simple tenses.

I (go) ...went... to London for the first time in 1970 when I (be) 1 .... just a child. My parents (already be) 2 .... there many times so they (know) 3 .... the city well. But they (never be) 4 .... there with a child, so they saw a different side of London with me. We (go) 5 .... out every day and (have) 6 .... a fantastic time. My parents (study) 7 .... English for many years so they (have) 8 .... no difficulty with the language. It (rain) 9 .... while we (be) 10 .... there, but we (pack) 11 .... all our waterproof clothes so it (be) 12 .... no problem. When the time (come) 13 .... to leave, I (feel) 14 .... quite sad because I (have) 15 .... such a good time.

GRAMMAR: the past tenses

2 Read the article from a local newspaper, then follow the instructions below.

100 YEARS OLD TODAY!

TODAY IS MRS MARY AMBLER'S one-hundredth birthday. Mrs Ambler is still living at 17 Laburnum Gardens, in the house where she has lived all her life. She says she has never wanted to live anywhere else. All her memories from childhood to old age are here in this house. She was a child here and then had her own three children here. All of them left many years ago and her daughters are now grandmothers. Mrs Ambler's husband died ten years ago, so she has lived alone since then. She never feels lonely, however, because she has many friends and relations who come to visit her.

The above article was written two years ago. Mrs Ambler has just died, and the journalist who visited her is writing another article, recalling what he said on her hundredth birthday. Write the new article in your notebook, changing the tenses and making any other necessary changes.

...Two years ago, on 1st June, it was Mrs Ambler's one-hundredth...
...birthday. She was still living at...

READING

3 Read the magazine article and answer the questions.

1 What is Mademoiselle Maigret's job?

....

2 Answer the questions, using the past perfect tense.
a) Why were there celebrations in Paris?

....

....

b) Who agreed to return the paintings to France?

....

....

c) What was dangerous about the house Mireille Balestrazzi walked into?

....

....

3 Underline all the examples of the past perfect tense in this article.

How many are there? ....

WEDNESDAY PEOPLE

Mademoiselle 'Maigret'

Mireille Balestrazzi: Corot-catching copper

THERE were celebrations in Paris yesterday when people heard that four stolen Corot paintings had been returned to France. They were brought back from Japan by France's most glamorous policewoman, Commissaire Mireille Balestrazzi.

The 33-year-old head of the Paris Arts Theft Squad, whose earlier successes had been the inspiration for a film starring Miao-Miao, was given a Madonna-style reception in Tokyo when she arrived in search of the stolen Impressionist paintings, including Monet's *Rising Sun*. After a short search, she found them. The people who had bought the four Corots in Japan agreed to return them to France.

Balestrazzi, the daughter of an army colonel and the wife of an army officer, has two sons. She was appointed a police inspector as soon as she had finished university, and at the age of twenty-five was made head of the Criminal Investigation Department in Creil. Her first big success occurred when she was called to a house where three armed criminals had hidden themselves after a robbery. She calmly walked into the house, took a gun out of her hand bag and arrested all three.

SPEECHWORK: pronunciation

Past perfect

4 Study the pronunciation, then listen to the tape and do the drills.

Had
Contraction = 'd
They'd left the tickets at home. / ðeɪd /

5 Listen and tick the sentences which you hear.

a) They've lived here for three years. ☑
b) They'd lived here for three years. ☐

1 a) Have you met her before? ☐
b) Had you met her before? ☐

2 a) We've had a lovely holiday. ☐
b) We'd had a lovely holiday. ☐

3 a) She worked there for a long time. ☐
b) She'd worked there for a long time. ☐

4 a) They walked all the way. ☐
b) They'd walked all the way. ☐

5 a) They hurt themselves. ☐
b) They'd hurt themselves. ☐

Unit 47

WRITING: *in spite of/although*

1 Match the sentences in Column A and Column B, then join them using *although* and *in spite of*.

A	B
I have a lot of friends	he's very boring to talk to
1 He had a heart attack last year	she can still look after herself
2 She's very old now	I sometimes feel lonely
3 He's very intelligent	he seems to be quite healthy
4 She works very hard	she doesn't earn much money

Although I have a lot of friends, I sometimes feel lonely.
In spite of having a lot of friends, I sometimes feel lonely.

1 ....
....

2 ....
....

3 ....
....

4 ....
....

VOCABULARY

2 Complete the sentences with different types of writer.

A *novelist*.......... writes novels.

1 A ....*p*.......... writes plays.

2 A ...*p*.......... writes poems.

3 An *a*.......... writes books.

4 A ..*j*.......... writes newspaper articles.

LISTENING

3 Listen to the book reviews and write which type of book the reviewer is talking about.

1 *thriller*	detective story
2	biography
3	autobiography
4	thriller
5	travel book
6	romantic novel
7	collection of short stories

Unit 48

COMMUNICATION: expressing regrets

1 **Rewrite these sentences, starting with *I wish*.**

I don't have a job. — *I wish I had a job.*

I didn't go to Rod's party last night. — *I wish I'd gone to Rod's party last night.*

1 We had an argument. ....

2 I can't speak English very well. ....

3 I didn't help them. ....

4 I have to go to school. ....

5 I don't live near a swimming pool. ....

2 **A month after writing the letter on the right, Adrian failed all his exams and had to leave university. Look at his letter, and imagine five things that he now wishes he'd done differently.**

I wish I hadn't gone to all those parties.

1 ....

2 ....

3 ....

4 ....

5 ....

I'm having a wonderful time at university. The social life is fantastic and you don't have to work very hard. I go to parties nearly every night and when there isn't a party, I spend the evening playing pinball. That means I usually go to bed pretty late but it's O.K. because I don't have to get up early in the mornings. There are lectures every day but I think most of them are a waste of time, so I don't bother to go. You're supposed to write an essay every week but nobody says anything if you don't give them in, so I stopped doing them after two weeks. I've got my first year exams next month but everyone says they're really easy so I don't think I'll need to do much revision – very few people get thrown out!

Anyway, why don't you come and stay? You'd have a great time.

Best wishes,
Adrian

SPEECHWORK: stress and intonation

Expressing regrets

3 **Study the stress and intonation, then listen to the tape and do the drills.**

I WISH the office was NEARer the STAtion.

I WISH I hadn't gone to BED so LATE.

Unit 49

GRAMMAR: the third conditional

1 Complete the sentences by writing the verbs in the correct form, using the third conditional.

If I (not get lost) *hadn't got lost*, I (not/meet) *wouldn't have met* her.

1 If it (not/rain) ...., I (go) .... to the park.

2 I (call round) .... if I (know) .... you were at home.

3 He (get) .... the job if he (apply) .... for it.

4 We (do) .... something about it if we (know) .... what was going to happen.

5 If he (not/see) .... that film, he (not/buy) .... a gun.

6 She (be killed) .... if you (not/be) .... there.

7 She (not/leave) .... if she (not/be) .... so unhappy.

GRAMMAR: first, second and third conditional

2 Complete the sentences, using the information in brackets and the correct conditional.

If I wake up early tomorrow, *I'll go for a swim before work.*
(go for a swim before work)

1 Would you buy these shoes ....
(have the money)

2 If I'd got home earlier, ...
(see them)

3 I could have got that job ....
(want it)

4 If she rings me again, ...
(I/tell her the news)

5 She'd be angry ....
(know about this letter)

6 We'll miss the train ....
(not hurry)

7 She might have done it for you ....
(you/ask her)

3 **Look at the advertisement on the right and answer the questions.**

1 Is the advertisement amusing or serious?

....

....

2 Rewrite the advertisement with an *if* clause.

....

....

WRITING

4 **Using the same idea as the advertisement above, write sentences for the products below.**

a Skyways' plane/get there faster

Christopher Columbus

would have got there faster in a Skyways plane.

1 a 'Techno' computer/find the answers more quickly

Albert Einstein

____

2 Allcure medicine/save more lives

Florence Nightingale

____

3 Goldmark designer clothes/ look more beautiful

Queen Victoria

____

4 'Clearview' glasses/ be able to see better

Sherlock Holmes

____

SPEECHWORK: pronunciation

The third conditional

5 **Study the pronunciation, then listen to the tape and do the drills.**

If <u>you'd</u> worked harder, <u>you'd have</u> passed your exams.
/ ju:d / / ju:dəv /

If <u>you'd</u> stayed at home, you <u>wouldn't have</u> been ill.
/ ju:d / / wʊdntəv /

Unit 50

GRAMMAR: question tags

1 **In Unit 50 of your Students' Book, Melinda says: '...... you can't read, can you?' Remember, *can you?* is a question tag. Complete the sentences with a question tag.**

It's a lovely day, isn't it ?

1 You went out last night, ...

2 You're coming next week, ...

3 You haven't met Derek, ...

4 You'll be twenty next birthday, ...

5 I shouldn't have said that, ...

6 He hadn't been there before, ...

7 We must get up early tomorrow, ...

8 She lives next door, ...

9 You weren't living here last year, ...

10 He's not going to stay with you, ...

WRITING

2 **In the reading passage in the Students' Book, Melinda was looking at a questionnaire. What do you think the first question was? Complete it in the questionnaire below and think of three more questions.**

Twenty questions to test if you're really in love

	Yes	No
1. Would you rather be with him ....?	☐	☐
2. ....?	☐	☐
3. ....?	☐	☐
4. ....?	☐	☐

BLUEPRINT QUIZ

3 **How much can you remember about *Blueprint*? See if you can answer the questions below.**

1 What is the name of the school that Nick goes to? ....

2 What does Nick want to be? ....

3 What is Angie's job? ....

4 Which part of London does Angie live in? ....

5 What town is Glenn staying in? ....

6 What famous person lived in this town? ....

7 What is Eve's job? ....

8 What is Avebury Ring made of? ....

9 What is Errol's favourite sport? ....

10 What happened when Errol and his girlfriend went to watch the Cup Final at Wembley?

....

Pronunciation index

Pronunciation table

Consonants *symbol*	*key word*	Vowels *symbol*	*key word*
b	back	iː	sheep
d	day	ɪ	ship
ð	then	i	happy
dʒ	jump	e	bed
f	fat	æ	bad
g	get	ɑː	park
h	hot	ɒ	hot
j	yet	ɔː	door
k	key	ʊ	put
l	like	u	situation
m	man	ʊ̯	ambulance
n	sun	uː	food
ŋ	sung	ʌ	cut
p	pen	ɜː	bird
r	red	ə	better
s	soon	eɪ	make
ʃ	fishing	əʊ	note
t	tea	aɪ	bite
tʃ	change	aʊ	now
θ	thing	ɔɪ	boy
v	view	ɪə	here
w	wet	iə	peculiar
x	loch	eə	there
z	zoo	ʊə	tour
ʒ	television	uə	factual
		eɪə	player
		əʊə	lower
		aɪə	fire
		aʊə	power
		ɔɪə	employer

Review of Speechwork pronunciation

1 Weak and strong forms

a) Most auxiliary verbs have a weak pronunciation form and a strong pronunciation form.

The weak form is generally used in:

1 *Questions*
Where do they work? /də/
Does he enjoy his job? /dəz/
Has he left yet? /həz/
Were they still eating? /wə/

2 *Positive sentences*
It was made in Japan. /wəz/

The strong form is generally used in:

1 *Negative sentences*
It wasn't made here. /wɒzənt/
They weren't very happy. /wɜːnt/

2 *Short answers*
Yes, they do. /duː/
No, she doesn't. /dʌzənt/
Yes, he has. /hæz/

(See Speechwork Units 2, 22 and 26)

b) The modal auxiliary verb *can* also has both weak and strong pronunciation forms.

The weak form /kən/ is generally used in:

1 *Questions*
Can you sing? /kən/
Who can you see? /kən/

2 *Positive sentences*
I can dance. /kən/

The positive strong form /kæn/ is generally used in:
Short positive answers
Yes, I can. /kæn/

The negative uses another strong form /kɑːnt/:
No, I can't. /kɑːnt/
I can't swim. /kɑːnt/

(See Speechwork Unit 14)

c) In the perfect form of modal verbs, *have* is usually pronounced in the **weak form** /əv/:
She might have gone home. /əv/
They must have left. /əv/
We shouldn't have told them. /əv/

(See Speechwork Units 36, 39 and 49)

d) *To* is generally pronounced in its **weak form** /tə/ when it is followed by a *consonant*:
It's going to rain. /tə/
We used to share a house. /tə/

It is generally pronounced in its **strong form** /tʊ/ when it is followed by a *vowel*:
When's the shop going to open. /tʊ/
He used to own a car. /tʊ/

(See Speechwork Units 9 and 12)

2 Contractions

Some auxiliaries have a **contracted form.** This is generally used in *positive sentences*:
They've gone out. /ðeɪv/
She's already done it. /ʃi:z/
He'll understand. /hi:l/
If you'd got up earlier, ... /ju:d/

It is also sometimes used in *negative sentences*:
She's not coming. /ʃi:z/

However, more frequently, the word *not* is contracted to *n't*:
... you wouldn't have missed the train. /wʊdntəv/
I won't do it. /wəʊnt/
They haven't arrived. /hævənt/
John isn't coming. /ɪzənt/

(See Speechwork Units 22, 32, 46 and 49)

3 Word linking

When two words are said quickly together, this sometimes changes the pronunciation of the two words.
What do you do? /dʒu/
Do you live here? /dʒu/
Where did you go? /dɪdʒu/
Did you enjoy it? /dɪdʒu:/

(See Speechwork Units 2 and 6)

Longman Group Limited
Longman House, Burnt Mill, Harlow,
Essex CM20 2JE, England
and Associated Companies throughout the world.

© Longman Group Limited 1995
All rights reserved; no part of this publication may be reproduced, stored in a retrieval system, or transmitted in any form or by any means, electronic, mechanical, photocopying, recording, or otherwise, without the prior written permission of the Publishers.

First published 1995
Second impression 1995
Set in 10/11½ pt Linotype Versailles 55
Printed in Spain by Mateu Cromo, S.A. Pinto (Madrid)

ISBN 0 582 27535 0

Designed by Glynis Edwards

Illustrated by Andrew Aloof, Michael Armson, Caroline Church, Jerry Collins, Terry McKivragan, David Parkins, Martin Salisbury

ACKNOWLEDGEMENTS

We are indebted to the following for permission to reproduce copyright material: Gruner & Jahr UK Ltd for extract based on information in article 'Enormous Walter has more than a slim chance of Success' & adaptation of article 'Woman of the Week: Sharon Sexton, West End nightclub bouncer and Minder' from *Best* Magazine 24-30 January, 1988. p7; Guardian Newspapers Ltd for extract based on information in article 'Mademoiselle Maigret' by Stuart Wavell from *The Guardian* 2.12.87.

The Publishers are grateful to the following for their permission to reproduce photographs:–
Associated Press for page 68; Berol Ltd., Kings Lynn, England (writing instrument and art material manufacturers and suppliers) for page 72; *Best* Magazine for page 56; British Railways Board for page 24; J. Allan Cash for page 27; Image Bank for page 65 right; David Keith Jones for page 20; Max Jones for page 44; Tony Stone for page 65 left.